SOLD AMERICAN!

SOLD AMERICAN!

Philippe J. Brossard

Introduction by
Percy W. Bishop

Peter Martin Associates Limited

Library of Congress Catalog Card Number: 75-174571
ISBN: 0-88778-060-1

Peter Martin Associates Limited, 17 Inkerman Street, Toronto, Ontario.

CONTENTS

To the Canadian workers —
  who are the backbone of the economy.

Acknowledgments

In the course of human events we become, one way or another, obligated to those whose efforts before us have established the footpaths of life we choose to follow.

In this sense I have accumulated many debts.

I owe a great debt to Canadian financier Percy W. Bishop. His deep concern for the country's economic dilemma encouraged me to start upon this book. His understanding of the financial structure of the country led me through one economic complexity after another.

To my publisher, Peter Martin, my debt is enormous. His advice, counsel and guidance through many difficult chapters helped to salvage an original text that might otherwise have remained unwieldy pages of political prose.

To newspapers, the daily documents of the society, I convey my gratitude. They have been the source of "literary kindlings" for many of the paragraphs in this book, and their libraries an important source for research.

To this list of aids I add, with thanks, Canadian radio and television stations, who for me have been an enormous information resource.

Nor can I fail to mention my indebtedness to the many members of public libraries, foreign embassies and government bureaus of statistics for their constant willingness to help.

My outstanding intellectual debt must certainly go to the members of the Metropolitan Toronto Central Library, Business Reference Division, on College Street. After wading through miriads of files of newspaper clippings, journals, notes, pamphlets and listings, I cannot but respect and admire such a disciplined order of information.

I wish to thank too, Gordon Divers and Ross Howard, whose journalistic experience punctured my literary ego severely in the earlier drafts. Their keen interest and advice is greatly appreciated.

These are some of the many footpaths I have followed, and some of the people who have helped me find my way. I am grateful to them all.

P.J. Brossard

INTRODUCTION

Canada's enemies are within, not without.

If Canadians are to save Canada, they must do what they have never done before. They must seek the truth.

They must realize that unless they regain and retain greater control of the economy, their political freedom will vanish. Criticizing the British, the French, the Japanese, or the 200 million Americans for owning a large part of our economy will not provide any defensive measures. The real culprits are some 1,000 Canadians who control the nation's financial machinery. They have been unwilling to finance Canada's industries and natural resources to the extent that would spell success for our economy.

We must *tear down* the walls that protect those of the financial fraternity who have sold the country out, and poured hundreds of millions of dollars of Canadians savings into Wall Street, the world's greatest casino.

Canadians must demand legislation that will channel finances into the development of Canada's economy, particularly its natural resources.

Philippe Brossard, author of *Sold American!*, has focussed upon the indisputable facts which show how this nation is rushing towards economic destruction.

His book is not concerned with an ideology. It is simply

a call for action to an ill-informed, confused, and misled society. Our indifference and lack of national pride allowed a few members of the industrial and financial establishment to carry out a programme of liquidation of the country.

The author has vividly portrayed the unforgiveable deterioration of our sovereignty and economic viability during the past fifteen years. He has warned us that we cannot sit idly by and expect the government to correct the wrongs which have been perpetrated by power groups. These groups, as most members of parliament can see, not only help finance political parties, but directly or indirectly shape legislation and policy towards selfish ends that strangle the growth of Canadian ownership and prevent development of our resources.

Philippe Brossard touches the nerve of the nation when with irrefutable evidence, he discloses the devious manoeuvering of many Canadian investment houses which direct the country's financial pipeline of Bay Street and St. James Street, to Wall Street, in the greatest financial manipulation ever to be recorded in human history. This foul collusion has left hundreds of thousands of Canadians and millions of Americans financially depressed with only false expectations that the high prices of their glamour securities will ever return. These expectations must soon vanish when it is realized that most of the speculative securities distributed during the contrived prosperity of the past decade will never rise again — even to half the price at which they once traded.

He discloses previously unpublished facts which expose the abuse of the Canadian people by many of the same elite who help to elect and control governments.

These abuses must end.

On April 20, 1970, Alan Abelson, in the American financial weekly, *Barrons,* had this to say:

By all signs, the skids are greased and it could be quite a slide. The reason, of course, is that unlike '62, what is being corrected is not merely a year or two of wild but traditional speculation. This time around, the air is oozing out of a balloon that carried quite a crew: "class" investment bankers who underwrote assorted collections of junk without batting an eye; commercial banks which lent their names and their dollars to the conglomerate craze; bank trust departments which liberally spiced their accounts with dubious stocks; mutual funds that sacrificed prudence on the altar of performance.

In short, in sheer eminence, there hasn't been anything like it since the twenties. How, then, could anyone really believe it would end with a whimper instead of a bang?

Many financial organizations and their analysts, undisturbed by the losses running into billions of dollars, have failed to help Canadians avoid being brainwashed by foreign and domestic investment companies. This brainwashing during the past fifteen years has changed a society confident in its own future, involved in its own development and admired throughout the world, into a nation permeated with disillusionment, defeat and despair, retaining little or no actual control over its economy.

Canadians have only a short period of time to avert fatal disaster — not ten years, not even five. The next Ontario provincial election, and next federal election, will decide the destiny of Canada.

Canadians must be alerted now.

Sold American! should be read by all Canadians who want to know what is happening to their country. It is time to rally all those who respect future generations; all those who wish to provide valid opportunities for the present population; all those who honour the hardship and suffering of the millions who have gone before, especially the more than 100,000 young men who died in two World Wars that Canada might live.

Percy W. Bishop

ESAU'S MISTAKE

They wrote a noble chapter in the book of man's history. Coming from many lands, they created a humane, tolerant and democratic society. They were loyal to their allies and valiant in battle, but they never waged aggressive wars. They explored their vast, rich, hostile land, developed its resources, and poured forth upon the world the bounty of their furs, their grain, their gold, their minerals. To knit their giant land into one fabric, they developed a unique capacity for combining public and private initiative, threw railways from one ocean to another, harnessed the surging power of their rivers to drive the machines of their mines and factories. They rewarded the venturesome, protected the weak. They built great cities across the land and created for themselves a way of life that was second to none in the world.

It's too bad their history was so short.

They were the Canadians and they could have been great.

But they made Esau's mistake. They sold their birthright for a mess of pottage. Through shortsighted greed and startling error, they allowed control of their resources and the direction of their destiny to pass beyond their borders. When they lost control of their economy, they lost control of their fate. They became dependent upon their giant neighbours to the south. They learned to kowtow. They lost their pride and they lost their future.

Remember that future? The Twentieth Century, one of our

1

great men told us once, belongs to Canada.

If he was right, then the future that belongs to us doesn't include the minerals of our northland. It doesn't include the oil and potash of our prairies. It doesn't include the factories of our industrial heartland.

Because the battle — and a battle it is — for Canada's economic independence is not only being rapidly lost — it is virtually over.

Canadians do not own their economy; they merely support it.

Canadians do not control their destiny; they merely accept it.

The once-distinctive Canadian character is being steadily eroded through continuous adaptation to the demands of American capital, American development and the Americans' own view of their destiny and the destiny of mankind. As we lose control of our economy, we lose the power to determine our own priorities, both personal and national; we lose our freedom to decide what is right and what is wrong, what is good and what is bad, in a world where free men must keep that freedom if they are to remain free.

We are, of course, not alone. The British and the French have seen American capital, American initiative and American ideas distort and redirect the heritage of a thousand years. American rice grows in the Philippines. Nigerians drink Coke on the shores of Lake Chad. Chevs and Plymouths labour up the Andes to Chichen Itza. IBM computers tell the Indian government about their growing population.

The USA's gross national product exceeds one *trillion* dollars a year. American astronauts practice golf on the Moon. Their multi-national corporations change the shape of the world's economy. Theirs is a power unimagined in world history. But behind the facade of their strength lies a hint of decadence.

And good or bad, we are their partners in both their

2

material triumphs and their moral failures.

And, all the while, other peoples are learning the American secrets — the management talents, the capital-marshalling techniques, the marketing skills. In Japan and around the Asian perimeter, hungry entrepreneurs are producing goods to American standards, at less than American prices. In the European Economic Community, soon to be joined by Britain, a new money power is arising to challenge American predominance. The US dollar is under pressure from the Mark and the Yen. The US balance of trade moves into the red. Here and there across the US, spot unemployment grows; newly aggressive foreign competition begins to hurt.

But still the US Behemoth bestrides the economy and the policy of the free world. It does so on the strength of inherited wealth, accumulated expertise . . . and Canadian raw materials. It is our resources and their huge production lines, in partnership, which have combined to dominate world markets for two decades.

But it's a partnership, as W.H. Pope says, of *The Elephant and the Mouse.* *

Unequal on the face of it. Even more unequal when you discover that the elephant *owns* the mouse.

And almost totally incredible when you discover that the elephant has been using the mouse's money to buy him out.

In spite of the three to four million dollars interest we pay every day on US loans; in spite of the continuing takeover of Canadian companies by Americans; in spite of the seemingly permanent cut-rate sale of our natural resources; in spite of the presence of more than forty American brokerage branches across Canada wooing Canadians to buy Wall Street securities; in spite of the reluctance of our own financial institutions to invest in Canadian undertakings; in spite of — or because of —

The Elephant and the Mouse, by W.H. Pope. McClelland and Stewart, Toronto, 1971.

all these things, we continue to supply the money that the Americans use to buy up our country. We erase, with every dollar, a portion of our own identity, steadily contributing to the obliteration of our independence.

In the pages that follow, we will try to avoid, as far as possible, the mathematical complexities of economic analysis*, but inevitably any discussion of such matters as ownership of industry and control of the economy must involve some figures. We cannot, for example, appreciate how much of our economy is already in foreign hands without looking at the figures. Here are a few of them:

Industrial Sector	Percentage of Foreign Control in 1966
Manufacturing	58
Petroleum and Natural Gas	73
Mining and Smelting	62

The figures in that brief table are for 1966. As we write, in 1971, the percentages of foreign control are higher. The erosion of Canadian control continues.

In each case, American control accounts for more than three-quarters of total foreign control.

In major parts of our "manufacturing" industries, the figures are even more startling:

Manufacturing	Percentage of Foreign Control in 1966
Automobiles & parts	96
Rubber	99
Transportation Equipment	80
Electrical Apparatus	78
Chemicals	80

*You'll find an annotated bibliography at the back of the book. Most of the titles listed involve a little effort on the reader's part. None needs a degree in economics to be understood. All the books listed will reward the serious reader.

Not since King Attalus III gave Pergamum to the Romans and made his people subjects of the Roman Empire, dependent totally upon decisions made in a foreign land, has there been a sell-out like the Canadian sell-out.

Can our factories manufacture trucks for China? No, because the factories are American-controlled and the Americans don't trade with China.

Can our millers grind flour for Cuba? No, because our millers are American-controlled and the Americans don't trade with Cuba.

Does our oil industry join forces with the nations of the Middle East to negotiate a better price for our sales to the Americans? No, because our oil companies are mostly American companies and our government cannot afford to offend the oil lobby in Washington.

Can International Widget of Canada Limited export widgets to the United States? No, because International Widget of Canada Limited is a controlled subsidiary of American Widget, Inc., and American Widget wants to keep the market for itself.

For that matter, can International Widget of Canada export to Afghanistan? Not a chance, if American Widget decides the Afghan market is to be served from the United States. And if the world-wide market for widgets contracts, guess who is laid off; the widget makers in Smith's Falls, of course, not the widget makers in Sanduski.

In a democratic society of free men, we assume that we have a meaningful degree of control over our own destiny. We have freedom of choice and can shape our own lives and careers.

Oh yeah?

Choose your breakfast cereal? For all practical purposes, your choice is limited to the products of the subsidiaries of two American companies, both of which are bombarding your children with seductive commercials attached to American programmes.

5

Choose a car suited to Canadian conditions? Your choice is limited to designs created to meet American needs — or, maybe, British or German or Japanese (there used to be independent Canadian car makers; there used to be a lot of things).

Canadians — the people who thought they were going to be heirs to the Twentieth Century — are today uniquely subservient to decisions made beyond our borders. A great trading nation, we call ourselves in those Chamber of Commerce speeches. Strip away the veneer of rhetoric and you find that we are people who have lost control of our own affairs, our own destiny.

THREE FUTURE HISTORIES

We can't rewrite the past, but it is possible to have an influence on the future. Decide to leave your rubbers at home and your feet get wet in the rain; wear them and your feet stay dry. Either way, you're influencing future events by the decisions you make now. Nobody this side of God can predict with certainty the implications of decisions made and actions taken now. But we can certainly have an effect on at least some parts of our future.

For Canadians, three futures are open. And they look like this:

FUTURE FIRST

It's easy enough to see, as we look back on recent events, that the handwriting was on the wall early in the 1970's. But apparently the Liberal governments of those years either didn't notice what was going to happen to Canada — or they didn't care.

At any rate, Pierre Trudeau has been living in South America for years now and he won't talk to the press, so there's no way of knowing whether or not he understood what he was getting the Canadians into.

But he should have understood, because events began to snowball during his years in power. In spite of a few brave speeches by Canadian politicians, the American government offered the carrot and brandished the stick and the Continental Energy Policy became a reality. Canadian production and consumption of oil, gas, coal and hydro power became totally subservient to American requirements.

At the same time, shortsighted Canadian taxation policies accelerated the rate at which Canadian companies were selling out to the US.

When the American Southwest finally ran out of water, the North American Water and Power Alliance which had first been suggested in the 1960's became a reality. Water from the northern half of the continent was diverted south and east to supply a parched US west of the Mississippi.

Finally, and inevitably, it became obvious that Canadian political independence was obsolete. Canadian governments were dependent upon New York money markets for their borrowing. Canadian workers had jobs, or didn't have jobs, at the discretion of the managers of the American multinational corporations. Canadians had no control over their natural resources. Canadian managers and executives found they had no future unless they worked for the giant American corporations. And the Americans, of course, had bought up all the attractive Canadian recreational land from the shores of Nova Scotia to the islands of Georgia Strait, which was only natural since they already owned the country's downtown office buildings and suburban shopping centres.

Of course, there were objections. Walter Gordon issued a statement. Mel Watkins wrote several articles. Some hotheads in Montreal were caught plotting to blow up the American Embassy and the Parliament Buildings. But most Canadians had the issues clearly explained to them by the newspapers and TV stations (which were, of course, dependent upon American advertising) and they knew what they had to do.

So, when the referendum was taken in 1982, Canadians voted overwhelmingly to join the United States. They felt that the Americans were unexpectedly generous in agreeing that Canada should be allowed to contribute five states to the

8

Union; that meant ten Senators out of one hundred and ten —
far from a majority, of course, but it did mean that people
from the new "north of forty-nine" states had an influence
on legislation.

Unfortunately, our influence wasn't sufficient to have the
boys from our states exempted from the draft. They're
fighting on the Chinese front along with all the rest of us
Americans.

FUTURE SECOND

I expect I'll die here in the Laurentians. That's why I'm writing this short report now. If, by any chance, the Americans
ever get tired and go home — if the war ends and I'm still
alive — I think I'll try to write a comprehensive history of
these remarkable years, but I don't expect that to happen, so
these brief notes will have to do.

At the beginning of the seventies nobody in his right mind
could have predicted what was going to happen. Oh sure,
there were a lot of Canadians unhappy about the "American
takeover". Shrill-voiced academics wrote books. There was
even a semi-respectable organization called the Committee for
an Independent Canada. And the guy in the street wondered
occasionally if things mightn't be better if the Americans
didn't have so much say about what went on in Canada. But
the government didn't seem much concerned and we were
still in the grip of Trudeaumania.

But things began to get very tough during Trudeau's second
term in office. *He* hadn't changed, but the people had. When
the new Conservative leader began to crisscross the country
preaching anti-Americanism, people came out to listen and
shout their approval by the tens and hundreds of thousands.
Some of the academics deplored the Leader's "charisma"
and suggested that he was a bad thing for democracy in
Canada ("not in the Canadian tradition" they said), and they
became especially unhappy when we began to wear our Maple
Leaf armbands.

For that matter, I myself wasn't really committed until a friend talked me into joining the attack on IBM headquarters. I enjoyed myself so much that afternoon that I realized I wanted to join the movement — and so I did.

The next couple of years were very exhilarating. Of course, we won the election in spite of the American money that poured in to support the Liberals. And the Leaders' programme was reasonable enough — expel all US citizens from Canada; expropriate all American-owned land and other assets in Canada; close the Seaway to American shipping; make it a criminal offense to read American books and magazines or listen to American broadcasts — I mean, things had gone so far that the Leader had to take firm measures to restore our independence — but the reaction of the Amerikans was so violent that of course the Leader had to close Parliament and suspend civil liberties (I personally thought it was strange that he jailed Trudeau; the man was, after all, completely harmless).

All trade between the two countries stopped two days after we closed the St. Lawrence to ships bound for Amerikan ports. The Amerikans, as usual, went to extremes. We were only trying to restore our sovereignty — we had nothing against them as people; some of my best friends are Amerikans — but they seemed to think we were part of some kind of Communist plot. Especially since the Russo-Canada Trade Pact had changed our trade patterns.

We didn't really expect what happened next. I mean, the Amerikans have always talked about people's freedom of choice and we have always been their best friends. But I guess they needed the Seaway too badly. And the nickel. And the Western oil and gas. And, for that matter, the dollars they took out of Canada.

But I was really surprised when they attacked. At first they just combined a naval blackade with pinpoint bombing on our ports (they seemed to be particularly anxious to close the West Coast ports; probably had something to do with our

China trade), and civilian casualties were very light. But when a few hotheaded Canadian "irregulars" blew up the court house in Stowe, Vermont, the Amerikans used that as an excuse to move against us in strength.

The First Cavalry (a tough outfit; battle-hardened in southeast Asia a few years back) boiled up Route 9 and took Montreal with little trouble. There was a little opposition from the Canadian Forces, but not enough for the First Cavalry to worry about; we couldn't do anything from the air because our whole defense communications system was tied into NORAD and, of course, they controlled that network.

After they took Ottawa we learned one of those curious little facts that makes life so strange: the Amerikan soldiers found the old Canadian Forces operational orders from the "Apprehended Insurrection" of 1970 and used them to develop the details of their pattern of occupation.

But, even so, the Leader escaped. I think he's in the second chalet down the hill as I write this. We rallied around him here in the Laurentians. When the Leader talks about how we are going to "liberate" Canada none of us takes him too seriously. I mean, that's just propaganda. It sounds good to the people in the cities when they listen to our mobile radio broadcasts, but there's no way we can actually *defeat* the Amerikans in open battle.

I'm sure the Leader knows this too. After all, he's getting us to follow the advice of the National Liberation Front advisors who've come in. Just keep harrassing the Amerikans with guerrilla tactics. Eventually they'll get tired and go home and we'll have our freedom back.

Especially because of the Black Revolution that's going on in their cities.

FUTURE THIRD

Would you believe there was once a time — in fact, as little as fifteen years ago — when a lot of Canadians were afraid

11

that the Americans were going to control our economy? I know it sounds absurd, but all you have to do is look at the books that were written, the speeches that were made, as recently as 1971.

For years the American investment in Canada had been building up until it reached the point where it could feed on itself; it could continue to grow from its own profits without any more new American money coming into Canada.

And it wasn't just profit that made the Americans interested in us. They needed our oil and gas, our minerals, our water and it seemed to them that the easiest and best way to get what they needed was simply to own our resources. After all, we had been their friends for a century and a half and they — and we — had always thought of "business" as being something that crossed borders in North America.

For a few years back then, there were real difficulties between us. We didn't like their wars in Asia, for example. We didn't like the restraints they placed on our export trade, the influence they had on such things as the availability of capital and jobs in Canada. And the real difficulty was that *they* didn't know *we* cared about these things; after all, we had never made an issue out of anything like this before. In the past, we had always worked things out so that both sides thought they were benefiting: The Columbia River Treaty; exemption from the "Guidelines" on American investment abroad; Lots of hardnosed bargaining, but no really fundamental disagreements.

But things began to change after the Liberal government of the early seventies undertook a serious, cabinet-level study of Canadian industry. For Canadians, that study meant that we were losing control of our own future as a result of American domination of our economy.

None of us thought we should stop trading with them. But most thoughtful Canadians, in all political parties, thought that there should be a few changes made.

The government recognized this grass-roots sentiment among the Canadian people and began to implement the recommendations of the study they had undertaken.

The Canada Development Corporation was created and played an active — and profitable — role in ensuring that Canadians kept control of their new resources, new enterprises.

Individual Canadians had always been interested in speculative investment, so tax laws were modified to make it a little more attractive for them to put their risk capital into Canadian enterprises, a little harder for them to put their speculative dollars at risk on Wall Street.

The "private" Canadian subsidiaries of large American corporations were required to offer a majority of their equity to Canadians. To their surprise, they discovered that this was not a particularly painful operation and that Canadians were willing to pay a good price for control of well-managed companies.

The Takeover Review Board was established in 1972. Surprisingly, it didn't have to actually *do* anything. Simply by examining and publicizing the facts surrounding each potential foreign takeover of a Canadian business, it brought Canadian buyers onto the scene. Of course, they were helped when the Canadian government modified its punitive position on the taxation of the cost of takeovers.

There were also a number of other measures that, almost unnoticed and imperceptibly, redirected the Canadian economy into Canadian hands. Most of these were buried at the bottom of the financial pages and none of them, in itself, made all that much difference. But their cumulative effect was enormous.

It turned out that the whole debate of the early 1970's was a Canadian phenomenon. The Americans didn't want to own Canada. They simply wanted what every reasonable businessman wants — the chance to make an honest profit on honest effort. Canadians had wasted a lot of time and effort deploring sinister American economic imperialism. When they actually sat down and produced policies and programmes to repatriate their economy, they found that the Americans thought this was perfectly reasonable.

And that's why we have full employment and a stable currency in Canada in the mid-eighties. The Americans are paying a fair price for what they get from us. And we are benefiting from access to their giant market. We keep the fruits of our own endeavour. Labour and management are free to negotiate their own agreements in Canada without a big brother looking over either shoulder. Risk capital for new resource development or industrial innovation is now readily available in this country. Standards of living continue to rise in an environment which has not been despoiled by short-sighted physical exploitation.

Our major problem at the moment is coping with the millions of people who want to come to live here.

That. And, of course, the American President's recent speech in which he expressed concern at the rate of takeover of American industry by Canadians.

One of the least expected, but most valuable, results of our peaceful recovery of our own economy must be the remarkable development of northern Ontario. Back at the beginning of the seventies the people of northern Ontario were getting such a bad deal that they were talking about creating a new province of their own. Their economy was built on mining, but the mines, as mines must, were being depleted and nothing permanent was being put in their place. Cobalt, a mining town, was already becoming a ghost and the handwriting was on the wall for the other municipalities in the Ontario north.

But when we recovered control of our own economy we seem to have simultaneously decided that a man had a right to live his life in the place he chose. In northern Ontario this was more sense than sentiment. Hydro power was available. Cheap, water-borne transportation was there. The base metals were at hand. It wasn't the easiest country on the face of the earth, but it was among the richest. So we invested the capital. Or rather we left some of the earnings there. Instead of stripping the ore bodies and abandoning the country, we diverted revenue into creating permanent communities. From North Bay to Sault Ste Marie a massive reinvestment programme was undertaken. It isn't finished yet, but it's remarkable to see what is happening to northern Ontario. People up there are talking about "the new Ruhr". Industry is moving in. The towns are growing. The mines and the steel mills and the power are providing the basis for a rich new industrial region. Fifteen years ago northern Ontario was dying and people up there were talking about forming an eleventh province. They're still talking about it, but now they're talking out of pride, not out of desperation.

There they are. Three scripts. Three futures for Canada. A few of the factors that go to determine our future are beyond our control — beyond any man's control. But most of the events that will shape the future, most of the ideas that will fuel the events, are dependent on what we do.

This book is about the third script, the third future. If we do nothing positive to influence our future, we will become part of the American Union. If we act out of fear and passion, we will find ourselves in violent conflict with our neighbours. But if we act firmly and with reason we can still play out the third script.

But first we must understand the events and forces that brought us to where we are today.

THE OVERSEERS OF ELDORADO

Canada has always been somebody's Eldorado.

Even before John Cabot sailed to Newfoundland with King Henry's charter, fishermen from southern Europe were scooping cod from the incredibly rich waters of the Grand Banks.

The French came to Canada as much for religious and political reasons as for economic gain, but it wasn't long before they discovered that Europeans would pay handsomely for the furs harvested in the cool wilderness of the Canadian interior.

When the British added Canada to their Empire, they found in our forests the tall masts and spars they needed to rig the ships that brought Napoleon to his knees and let Britannia rule the waves.

Grain from the newly-cleared, virgin fields of Upper Canada fed the English, and made beer and whiskey for the Yankees.

After the railroad was flung across the Prairies and Sir Clifford Sifton populated the empty plains, Canadian wheat fed the world.

Gold from the Cariboo and the Yukon helped finance a vast expansion of international trade and commerce.

In this century, silver, nickel, zinc, copper, asbestos and two dozen other, more exotic, minerals were wrested from the hard and ancient rock of the Canadian Shield to make possible the industrial technology of the twentieth century.

And the paper mills that fed on our great forests and our

seemingly limitless supply of clean, fresh water made the Western World literate.

Since the Second World War, new riches have been discovered in Canada. The vast iron mountains of Labrador now feed the mills of Pittsburgh. Oil and gas from our Prairies supply energy for the American midwest. Coal from the eastern slopes of the Rockies fuels the Japanese "economic miracle".

There are, even now, only twenty-two million of us, but we inhabit a vast treasurehouse, an Eldorado of the West. Canada as a political power has rarely stood tall on the world stage. But Canada, as a source of material wealth, has been a major factor in world history for almost five centuries.

We have always worked hard to meet the world's demand for our products and, until recently, we have been adequately rewarded for our efforts. We built a free and independent nation on the richness of our land and the strength of our people.

But, in this generation, we have seen our rights in this great Eldorado pass, with astonishing speed, into foreign hands.

The Americans have found *their* Eldorado. In Canada. Like Caesar, they came, they saw and they conquered.

And we didn't resist.

How did this happen? How did we lose our rights to the land we had found and developed? The answer is not simple. The facts involved are complicated, and they have been rendered almost impenetrably obscure by the myths that have come to surround the subject.

But if we are to have any future at all as a people, we must understand the facts, strip away the myths, determine the steps we must take to make the changes we want to make — and then take those steps.

Along the way, it's necessary to identify the heroes and the villains. The heroes aren't too hard to find. They are all those intrepid men, from the earliest explorer to the most contemporary entrepreneur, who have believed that Canada's potential was virtually unlimited, that hard work, ingenuity, a willingness to take risks, and a little luck were the elements needed to create new enterprises. It is men like these, who risked their reputations, their resources and even their lives to find and develop the resources of this nation.

But the villains in the story are obscured behind the veils of myth. We will have to dig a little deeper to find them. Some of them are very visible, but they masquerade as heroes. Others shun publicity of any sort and hide behind a barrier of wealth and power.

Throughout history, no one has been more vicious, more greedy, than the overseer of the great lord's estate. Afraid of his master, upon whom he depends, the overseer will go to any lengths to see that the lord is satisfied with the wealth generated by the estate. But the overseer is demanding on his own account, too, and learns to lie and steal to an extravagant degree; as long as the master stays happy, the overseer can do anything he wants with the people and resources of the estate.

The vicious overseer still rides, whip in hand, on the pampas of the great *latifundia* of South America.

In Canada, he isn't quite so ostentatious. But you will find him clustered, drinking his Chivas Regal, behind the drawn curtains of such institutions as the Mount Royal and St. James Clubs in Montreal, the York in Toronto, the Manitoba in Winnipeg, the Ranchman's in Calgary, the Vancouver in Vancouver — and the Rideau Club in Ottawa.

Because the truth is that the men who have sold Canada, the men who have become the overseers in this Eldorado of the West, the men who serve the foreign masters and line their own pockets generation after generation, these are the members of our social and economic elite, the people at the top of John Porter's "Vertical Mosaic".

In 1957, Professor Porter first identified the economic

18

elite in Canada in a study of the "907 Canadian resident directors of 170 dominant corporations in the Canadian economy.* These 907 individuals shared 1,304 out of a total of 1,613 directorships in the dominant corporations, 119 out of 203 (58%) of the directorships in nine chartered banks; 78 out of 134 (58%) in the ten largest Canadian life insurance companies.

John Porter found 127 members of his elite "at the head of financial institutions"; 23 senior executives of the chartered banks, 10 senior executives of the life insurance companies and 94 "investment bankers, stockbrokers, heads of trust companies, and promoters acting through holding companies". "Like the lawyers," he says, "the investment bankers, stockbrokers, and promoters interlock extensively . . . the 94 have altogether 181 directorships in the dominant corporations, 29 in the banks, and 11 in the life insurance companies."

When it comes to the question of actual power in the Canadian economic structure, Porter has this to say about the members of the elite who are active in the investment community: "Investment houses, and in some cases affiliated brokerage offices, are the nuclei from which partners acquire directorships in a variety of corporations. There are fourteen groups of partnerships comprising thirty-nine persons within the group of 94. One group of associates has seventeen directorships, another sixteen, and a third has fourteen. . . . Within the financial group there is an additional area for interaction in the stock exchanges, particularly of Toronto and Montreal, and in the Investment Bankers Association. . . . "

Twenty-two million Canadians are now manning an economy with a gross national product of eighty billion dollars a year — eighty billion dollars worth of goods and services.

But the economy is managed, if we accept Porter's portrait of the economic elite, by less than a thousand men who have

---

*"The Economic Elite and the Social Structure in Canada" by John Porter. *Canadian Journal of Economics and Political Science,* August 1957.

a stranglehold on the centres of economic power and decision-making in the nation.

The economic elite does not, of course, people the political institutions of the country. A few of them turn up in the House of Commons or the provincial legislatures. More appear in the Senate. And many serve from time to time on various governmental task forces, commissions and committees. In his very important full-scale study, *The Vertical Mosaic*,* John Porter demonstrates the role that "elite" lawyers serve by building a bridge between the economic elite and our elected representatives. Porter seems to conclude that, in spite of occasional conflict, the economic elite is satisfied with at least our two major political parties. The Liberals and the Conservatives do not, it appears, interfere too frequently or too vigourously with the activities and objectives of the economic overseers of our nation.

It is, of course, significant that a very large percentage of the funds the major political parties need to operate on and to campaign with comes in the form of donations from major corporations — the corporations that are managed by the thousand men Porter describes.

If we grant that Porter is right — that the "economic elite" determines the fate of the Canadian economy and that the political establishment acquiesces in this exercise of power by the economic leaders — then we can see very clearly who has sold our Eldorado to the foreigners.

They have sold us out at cut-rate prices. They have stayed on, in very comfortable circumstances, to manage the property they have sold.

Their job as overseers, of course, is to keep us productive and not too discontented. Their rewards are power, influence and wealth — the wealth they are granted by the real owners and the extra wealth they manage to wring for themselves from the property they are managing.

*The Vertical Mosaic, by John Porter. University of Toronto Press, Toronto, 1965.

It's an ugly picture wherever you see it in world history. Unfortunately, it's the picture of our society and our economy.

The strange political career of Walter Gordon throws a vivid light on the whole ugly scene. Gordon was clearly, by background and career, a member of the "economic elite". He entered politics as a Liberal and rose to Cabinet rank. He believed that Canadians should recover ownership of their own economy and he attempted to introduce programmes to achieve this objective. Immediately he was identified as a traitor to his class, was vilified in the press and from speaker's rostrums across the country, was thwarted in his legislative programs and, finally, was forced from his position of power and influence in the cabinet. Unrepentant, the Honourable Walter L. Gordon has now organized the Committee for an Independent Canada which is campaigning vigourously. He has also written a book about his political career; because of pressures from his family and his friends within the Liberal Party, Gordon has not yet consented to have the book published. He should.

It is now necessary to examine *how* our country was sold. And that is the subject of the next chapter.

SOLD...AMERICAN!

Adolf Hitler might have been talking about us when he said, "The great masses of the people will more easily fall victims to a great lie than to a small one." Because it is certainly the "great lie" that kept us quiet while our country was sold out from under us.

The great lie, of course, is that we *had* to sell Canada if we were to see our resources developed and enjoy a high standard of living for ourselves. The raw materials were here, as everyone knew, vast deposits of untouched, unexploited resources, but it was going to take capital to find and develop them, capital we didn't have.

Stanley Randall, Ontario's very vocal former Minister of Trade and Development, distinguished himself as a spokesman for those of us who believe the great lie.

Randall's statements are more vigourous, forceful and direct than those of most apologists for the foreign presence in Canada (in fact, Mr. Randall has been altogether one of our most entertainingly outspoken politicians; it's hard to agree with him, but it's even harder to be bored by him). Here are extracts from a speech he made to a Seminar on the Economics of Progress at the Annual Meeting of the Ontario Progressive Conservative Association in 1969:

> Straight off, I want to say that I'm for foreign investment in Ontario, and as long as I'm Minister of Trade and Development, I'm going to get *all* the investment I

can for the province. We have too many economic weirdos rushing into print today, doing their damndest to reduce Canada to the status of a banana republic . . . .

Now, personally, I think the problem of U.S. influence in Canadian companies is overstated. When you look at the *total* Canadian economy, foreign investment is not that significant . . . .

In certain sectors — such as manufacturing and mining — foreign investment is vital. In those sectors, we need large inputs of investment capital to create jobs and income. And though I acknowledge we have lost some freedom of action in an economic sense, we have not lost our political independence. By any manner or means, we're not owned by anybody. Government in Canada is responsible to Canadians.

In a letter to the *Toronto Star* some time later, Mr. Randall summed up his position by saying, "You don't need to be anti-Canadian to be pro-foreign."

Stanley Randall and other Upper Canadians who echo his views aren't the only people who continue to believe in and mouth the great lie. In Western Canada the same song is sung.

Interviewed on the CBC-TV program, *Encounter,* Premier Harry Strom of Alberta had this to say on February 25, 1971:

As a westerner, I can say without hesitation that we have only been able to enjoy the measure of prosperity that we have in Western Canada by foreign investment and the kind of development that we're looking at in the future demands that we still have that kind of investment in the development of our country.

And, speaking in Dallas, Texas, on March 9th, 1971 (to the Dallas section of the Society of Petroleum Engineers), the Hon. Jean Chrétin, Minister of Northern Development, said:

At the present time, some Canadians are asking them-selves if there are ways of increasing their own invest-ments in their own country, or if present controls are adequately protecting Canadian interests. The point I want to emphasize is that foreign capital need not fear such questioning, for we will remain an open country, seeking positive, not negative, answers to these question.

Behind the politicians and the corporate overseers stands the grand *guru* of the internationalists, Canadian born and educated Harry Johnson, professor of economics at the London School of Economics and, simultaneously, at the University of Chicago. Professor Johnson was noticeably quiet for many months while nationalist economists such as Professor Abraham Rotstein of Toronto challenged, both implicitly and explicitly, Johnson's views. But Johnson, as events revealed, had not given up. He was simply biding his time, waiting for the right platform and the right audience. He found them, early in May, 1971, at a meeting of the Ontario Institute of Management Consultants in Toronto.

"The Canadian economic nationalist movement," Professor Johnson said, "has focussed on the largely irrelevant issue of the ownership of industrial capital . . . the distressing thing about Canadian economic nationalism is the archaic 19th-century view of capitalism that somehow seems to comfort Canadian economic nationalists in the belief that they are abreast or ahead of — and not just colonially lagging behind — the 20th century . . . . "

After attacking both nationalists on the right and nationalists on the left, Johnson went on to say:

The 20th century view of capitalism, shared by eminent thinkers ranging all the way from the extreme left to the extreme right, but apparently unknown to Canadian economic nationalists of whatever persuasion, is that property ownership *per se* is pretty well irrelevant.

What matters for the efficiency and well-being of an economy is not who owns the property, but how efficiently and progressively it is managed . . . .

About the only positive virtue one can attribute to the nationalist agitation in Canada in the past 15 years is that it has obliged non-nationalistic pragmatic Canadians, and particularly Canadian economists, to rethink and restudy in depth the functions and benefits of private industrial competition . . . .

Turning from the politics to the economics of foreign investment in Canada, I agree with the broad finding of native Canadian scholarship that all the important problems that can be found are attributable to Canadian economic policy, or the lack of a Canadian economic policy, toward Canadian industrial enterprise in general — particularly to the tariff and to the weakness of Canadian anti-combines policy . . . .

While someone has to make the investment required to produce new industrial knowledge, there is an open question whether Canada does better by letting the large US corporations and the US government develop new industrial knowledge and make it available afterward at relatively low cost for Canadian producers and consumers, or would do better by promoting the development of more finely turned new knowledge in Canada at Canadian public expense. The latter process, if not well managed, could be both expensive and unproductive . . . . ''

Harry Johnson's mastery of the *non sequitur,* the *argumentum ad hominem* and other time-honoured sophistical tricks of argument is as impressive in its own way as is Stanley Randall's colourful invective. (Johnson showed his own talent for invective in the title of his talk: "From Gordon to Watkins to Uselessness".) Both men, although wrong, are certainly more interesting than the usual branch-plant corporate president who feels compelled to state the case for the multinational corporation and the Canadian sell-out.

Gene E. Roark, president of Husky Oil Limited, says that restriction of foreign investment in Canadian enterprises, "would appear to be mistaken economic nationalism". (Husky of Canada, with stated assets of better than $250 million, is controlled in the US.)

W.O. Twaits, president of Imperial Oil Limited, recently told the Association of Canadian Advertisers that opponents of foreign investment cannot accept the fact that to a Maritimer, a dollar of investment from Ontario is just as much foreign investment as a dollar of investment from the United States or Europe; that private investment is much more acceptable than government handouts; and that private investment carries with it market responsibility.

And listen to W. Earle McLaughlin, chairman and president of Canada's largest chartered bank. Speaking in New York in March, 1971, he said:

> Profits are earned by carrying out economic activity to meet economic needs and are a measure of performance. Foreign investment is the only reason there are any profits at all, in some cases, and in other cases foreign companies have to try harder. . . . Profits paid to foreigners are a measure of the services Canadians have received from foreigners. The greater the profits, the greater the services and the greater the Canadian tax revenues.

While Mr. McLaughlin welcomes foreign investment in Canada and cheers for the profits that foreign corporations earn in Canada, it's interesting to remember that Mr. McLaughlin's own industry — banking — is almost totally protected from foreign "branch plant" competition in Canada.

The federal Government gets into the act too. A full-page ad appearing in the prestigeous American business magazine, *Fortune,* early in 1971 asked: "Where on Earth Can you Get $12,000,000 for Creating New Jobs?" The answer appeared beneath an outline map. "In Canada, of course. The Government of Canada is prepared to pay cash grants of up to $12,000,000 (or a maximum of $30,000 for each job created) to companies establishing new plants in designated regions of Canada. The purpose is to encourage manufacturing and processing industries to start new activities and create new jobs in parts of Canada where they are needed."

Canadian-owned companies, presumably, are also eligible for the federal bounty, but it's significant that the advertisement appears in a magazine that's read by the captains of American industry.

Nobody is opposed to more jobs in Canada. Our chronic rate of unemployment is a disgrace for a country as rich and as productive as this one. But the great lie claims that the solution to unemployment is to be found in the further importation of foreign capital, the further transfer of control of our economy to foreigners. In fact, as we have hinted already, the dominant position of foreign capital in the Canadian economy is a major *cause* of chronic unemployment in Canada.

What are the facts? It *does* take capital to develop the economy, increase productivity, generate new jobs. Everybody knows this. You can't build a house if you don't have any money. If you don't have the money to build the house, there won't be jobs for house-builders. You can't drill an oil well if you don't have the capital to pay for the drilling; if you don't drill the well, you won't find the oil.

The question is where the capital — the money needed to get things done — can come from. Stanley Randall and other proponents of the great lie would have us believe that it must come from beyond our borders.

But that's just not true. It might have been true once upon a time — we borrowed money in London to help build the C.P.R. — but it isn't true now and it hasn't been true for years.

In her enormously important book, *Silent Surrender,** Professor Kari Levitt of McGill University uses figures from the *U.S. Survey of Current Business* to show that, "Over the

*Silent Surrender, Kari Levitt. Macmillan, Toronto, 1970.

years 1957 to 1965, 85 percent of the funds used to expand US-controlled industry in Canada was provided from Canadian domestic savings. More specifically, US subsidiaries in Canada obtained 73 percent of their funds from retained earnings and depreciation, and a further 12 percent from other Canadian sources, and only 15 percent from the United States."

"Retained earnings" are the profits made by the American-controlled companies that were kept in Canada to finance the companies' expansion instead of being paid out as dividends to the shareholders. "Depreciation" is money generated by making use of the land, equipment and buildings the company already owns.

From one source and another, *we* provided 85% out of every dollar *they* used to take over a larger and larger part of our economy.

And what have they been taking over? A partial list, "recorded annually by the Office of the Director of Investigation and Research under the Combines Investigation Act from press and other public reports concerning only industries under the jurisdiction of the Act (and excluding firms whose activities do not fall within the scope of the Act)" shows no fewer than 606 takeovers between 1963 and 1969, an average of close to one hundred Canadian businesses a year!

Do you like chocolates? Moirs and Jenny Lind and Walter M. Lowney and Laura Secord were all taken over (Laura Secord has subsequently returned to Canadian hands).

Or beer? The giant South African conglomerate, Rothmans, managed to snatch control of Canadian Breweries away from the US tobacco giant, Phillip Morris, in a fierce proxy battle.

Dozens of oil exploration companies were taken over as foreigners rounded out their almost total control of oil exploration and development in Canada. Occidental Petroleum got Jefferson Lake Petrochemicals. B.P. Canada Limited (largely British) got City Service Oil Company. Union Oil took over Pure Oil. British American Oil Company (subsequently renamed Gulf Canada) acquired Royalite Oil.

There's money to be made in selling food to Canada's growing population. That's why Bick's Pickles and Black Diamond Cheese and Clark Foods passed into foreign hands, as did the "mass-feeding" catering firms, Versafood Services and Canterbury Foods.

The Copp-Clark textbook publishing house was lost to Canadians, as were, in 1970, the Gage Textbook Division and the Ryerson Press, thereby ensuring that our children will learn most of their lessons — including Canadian history and geography and social studies — from books published by foreign-controlled firms. Even "francophone" Canadian children learn their lessons from books published by American subsidiaries; Encyclopedia Britannica acquired, in 1968, *le Centre de Psychologie et de Pedagogie,* the largest Quebec-based educational publisher.

If you buy bargain clothes, you might pick them up at Stedman's, which became a subsidiary of Gamble-Skogmo of Minneapolis in 1964. But if you prefer to spend more money on your wardrobe you might choose to shop at Holt Renfrew, which became a subsidiary of C.I.T. Financial Corp. in 1965.

The list seems endless. Besides the more-or-less well-known companies mentioned above, there are literally hundreds of takeovers of other firms in every field of human endeavour, from computers to funeral homes, from instrument makers to dairies, clothing manufacturers, snowmobile manufacturers, furniture manufacturers, stationery firms and papermakers and trucking companies and vintners and rope makers and steel makers and gravel pits and airplane leasing companies and finance companies and pharmaceutical companies and drive-in theatres and paperbag makers and makers of printing ink and tacks and fertilizers and pizza crusts and medals and barrels and gauges and coolers and typewriter ribbons and fuses and boats and . . . and . . . and . . .

Six hundred and six companies officially known to be lost in seven years, hundreds of others on which statistics were not compiled (and isn't it remarkable that our own Federal Government doesn't even keep a full and comprehensive list of the Canadian enterprises that pass to foreign hands?)

In a slightly different context, Campbell Hughes, the genial president of the US-dominated Canadian Book Publishers Council, underlined the internationalization of our economy by saying:

> A Canadian is someone who drinks Brazillian coffee from an English teacup, and munches a French pastry while sitting on his Danish furniture, having just come home from an Italian movie in his German car. He picks up his Japanese pen and writes to his member of Parliament to complain about the American takeover of the Canadian publishing business.

Mr. Hughes makes his point. But he would have made it more accurately if he had used the word "American" in place of all the other national adjectives in his whimsical description of the Canadian.

Because it is largely the Americans who have taken over the hundreds of companies that supply the profitable products and services that Canadians depend upon. And most of the money the Americans have used to take over these companies has come from Canada and Canadians.

But, incredible as it may seem to Stanley Randall and Harry Johnson and the others who believe that we *need* American money, while we were providing eighty-five percent of the money needed for Americans to buy up Canadian enterprises, *we were also investing hundreds of millions of dollars in the US.*

And that is where the great lie is exposed for what it is.

We are *not* short of capital.

We *do not need* massive foreign investment in order to develop our own economy.

The incredible, almost-suppressed truth is that we are exporting more capital to the United States than we are importing from them.

In the fourteen years from 1950 to 1964, the Americans invested $5,907,000,000 in Canada — but during the same period they took back from Canada $5,914,000,000. The net effect of all that foreign capital investment many Canadians have been so eager to attract is that the Americans took seven million dollars more *out* of Canada than they put in during those fourteen years.

Since 1964, the outflow to the US has accelerated. Dividends, license fees, royalties, management fees all flow back to the US from the operations of American subsidiaries in Canada. (American subsidiaries don't send back all their profits; Professor Kari Levitt reports that the Dominion Bureau of Statistics has estimated that the undistributed earnings of US subsidiaries in Canada for the nineteen years between 1946 and 1964 totalled $5.2 billion. The Americans used these funds to expand and diversify their operations in Canada; this is part of the price we haven't been billed for yet, but we'll have to pay it some day soon!)

While the Americans were generating enormous earnings for themselves in Canada and actually taking more money out of our country than they were putting into it, what were we doing with our investment dollars?

Between 1961 and 1967, we were net purchasers of $545 million worth of US securities and we were also buying back from foreigners (not all Americans) $792 million worth of the securities of Canadian companies.

We don't *need* foreign capital in this country. Canadians are great savers. In 1967, Canadians saved almost 9% of their disposable, after-tax income. The comparable figure for the US was just over 7%. Net savings at the rate of 9% of disposable income generate enough money every year to finance an economic growth rate almost as impressive as Japan's (the

Japanese are worried; their growth rate has *slowed down* to about 10% a year — mostly because there aren't enough workers to fill the jobs that are open in Japan).

Our perverse ingenuity is the marvel of the world. No other people could perform the feats of economic magic that the Canadians have pulled off. Nobody else in the world could produce and save as much as Canadians do and still manage to lose control of their economy and suffer from chronic unemployment and underemployment.

But then, the "great lie" is a uniquely Canadian bit of economic wisdom. No other people on the face of the earth could be persuaded to swallow such nonsense.

We are faced now with two seemingly irreconcilable facts.

First, this rich and productive nation generates enough capital to finance its own development, make its own decisions, control its own destiny.

Second, we do *not* control our own economy or our own destiny.

How this shameful situation developed is the subject of the following chapters.

TWO HUNDRED YEARS
OF AMERICAN HISTORY

Two hundred years of American history? But this book is about Canada.

Yes. Of course. But you can't understand the Canadians without understanding the role that the United States plays — and has always played — in their lives.

The "Conquest" of 1763 brought British and French together in an uneasy partnership in the northern half of North America. Before any acceptable accommodation could be worked out, a new crisis loomed: the American Revolution.

Seeking their own independence from Britain, the Americans attacked the territories that had remained loyal to the Crown. To the rebels' amazement, *les Canadiens* preferred British rule to the dubious pleasures of citizenship in the new republic to the south (the Montreal merchants wanted to join the U.S. — a foretaste of things to come!) Benedict Arnold retreated from Quebec in something resembling a disarray.

Sixty years later, when Britain was fighting for her very survival against the totalitarian ambitions of Napoleon, the Americans tried again. The aggressive, still-new republic declared war on Britain (one is reminded of Mussolini's 1940 attack on France; Hitler was beating France to her knees, so Mussolini moved in to share the spoils. In the War of 1812, a similar ambition failed; unfortunately for the Americans, Britain didn't lose to Napoleon and there were no spoils to carve up.) Again the Americans invaded British North America. They burned Muddy York (many Canadians have wanted to do the same since), but their achievements were more symbolic than lasting. *Canadiens* and Canadians alike rallied to defeat the invaders; the inhabitants of British North America were far from certain about what they wanted to be, but they knew without a doubt that they *didn't* want to be Americans. The invaders were repulsed. British troops burned Washington in retaliation. And the war, as wars do, dragged on to a conclusion, having done no one any good.

Lower Canada kept its own counsel, pursued its own special destiny. It was different and was determined to remain different. Lord Elgin reported back to Westminster that he had found "two nations warring in the bosom of a single state". Canadians, ever since, have read that to mean that there was conflict between French and English in the Canadas, and so there was. But, unstated and unnoticed, the more important fact is that *neither* of the nations wanted to become part of the republic to the south.

In both Upper and Lower Canada, there was a wide measure of discontent with things as they were. Family Compact and Chateau Clique and rule from the Colonial Office seemed inappropriate — even evil — to a vigorous, growing people. But, much as the Canadians resented their lack of popular democracy, they didn't want to associate themselves too closely with the strange ideas and events that were being spawned south of the border. There, popular democracy looked like tyranny of the majority. There, rule by the people looked like rule by the rabble. There, the institutions of society — often foolish, occasionally evil, but frequently protective of the rights of minorities — were swept aside on the impulse of the moment. Canadians, in 1860 as much as now, were fascinated by the "Great Experiment" of American republicanism, but were determined not to involve themselves in its excesses, its inhumanities. Canadians, discontented as

34

they were with the effete, authoritarian, decadent and inefficient rule they were saddled with, nevertheless wanted to solve their own problems. For the most part, they found serious violence repugnant (a little drunken battling around the polling booth was one thing; institutionalized killing was quite another). Thus ordinary citizens and leaders alike, in the separate and almost defenceless colonies of British North America, watched with increasing uneasiness as the Americans slaughtered one another by the hundreds of thousands in the ferocious War Between the States.

By 1865, the North was victorious and the Canadians found themselves living next door to the world's largest standing army, an army that had emerged triumphant from five years of bloodletting.

England, meanwhile, was continuing to suppress the ambitions of Irish nationalists and many Irish in the US thought they could break England's stranglehold on Ireland by assaulting the colonies of British North America. The Fenians mobilized south of the border and three times invaded Canada.

The Canadians, as every school boy knows, confederated into the new Dominion of Canada in a direct and specific response to the threat from the south.

Canadians' fear of the US and distaste for the political and economic habits of the "Yankees" remained alive for the balance of the nineteenth century. Anti-Americanism, plus something new — Canadian patriotism — led to Sir John A. Macdonald's "national policy" of 1878. The issues were enormously complicated in detail and the implications of this new policy were seriously misunderstood, but the questions were capable of sufficient simplification to become a genuine election issue: should Canada's economy grow through "reciprocity", which would integrate Canada's economy with that of the US and allow us to share in the Americans' burgeoning prosperity? (From the end of the Civil War, the

US had been industrializing and growing richer at a rate which astonished the world.) Or, alternatively, should Canada grow by erecting such high tariff barriers that foreign goods would be effectively shut out of Canadian markets, thereby creating an environment in which Canadian industry might grow to serve the Canadians' appetite for manufactured goods?

The people of Canada chose the latter alternative. Macdonald's "national policy" was endorsed. The tariff went up. And Canadian industry began to grow.

From the perspective of the times, the results were everything that Macdonald had hoped. After the turn of the century the Prairies filled up with settlers and the new grain farmers presented a rich and demanding market for manufactured goods. New factories in Ontario and Quebec churned out a multitude of products to meet the growing demand. Under the "national policy", the basic shape of Canada's contemporary economy was sketched.

But early in the twentieth century a new and perhaps unexpected result of the creation of a hothouse manufacturing economy in Canada began to appear.

Ambitious and expansionist American industrial corporations, unable to sell into the Canadian market from their home base because of the Canadian tariff, decided to share the Canadian wealth by establishing "branch plants" in Canada. (They were further motivated by the fact that a Canadian branch plant gave them easy access to British Empire, later Commonwealth, markets.)

Some firms simply moved in and set up shop; Henry Ford had only to cross the Detroit River to create Ford of Canada in Windsor.

Others took a less direct route; General Motors worked with and eventually acquired control of a vigourous, previously Canadian, firm; the McLaughlin Motor Car Company had by 1907 made the switch from horses to horsepower with intelligence and competence. To strengthen their position in

Canada, they made licensing arrangements with General Motors to distribute widely-advertised and efficiently designed GM cars in Canada. The relationship was, by its very nature, not an equal one and GM acquired control of McLaughlin in 1918. Colonel Sam McLaughlin, a great Canadian industrialist, became a multimillionaire by selling his company to General Motors. Almost to the Second World War, the McLaughlin name remained as a kind of public relations anachronism in the world of Canadian motoring. There were thousands of McLaughlin Buicks on Canadian roads, but the cars were Buicks, pure and simple, in all but name.

The story could be repeated in a thousand industries and it is still going on (see the selected list of recent American take-overs in Chapter 4).

The "national policy" had succeeded in its objective of filling the Canadian heartland with factories — but the factories were owned by Americans, their products were American products.

Of course, because Canadian markets were small, because the tariff protected Canadian factories from direct competition from abroad, and because every American firm wanted to build a factory in Canada if its competitors had done so, Canadians ended up paying astonishingly high prices for their goods. A multitude of small and inefficient factories in Canada turned out an absurdly uneconomical range of products.

It need not have been so, and a glance at one industry where the tariffs of the "national policy" did not hold permanent sway will serve to show what Canada's industrial economy *might* have been like.

From the start, Western farmers were opponents of high tariffs. They were selling their grain on world markets and at world prices and they resented being forced to buy manufactured goods from eastern Canadian factories at the high, protected prices that prevailed in Canadian secondary industry.

They were not able to change the direction in which Macdonald had pointed Canada, but they did score one victory: farm machinery was comparatively unprotected by tariffs. Canadian farmers could buy tractors and reapers and combines at close to world prices and not at inflated Canadian prices.

The Americans in the farm equipment industry had no compulsion to erect "branch plants" in Canada — they could ship and sell their products directly to Canadian buyers.

And, obviously, any Canadian firm that wanted to succeed in the farm equipment business had to meet and match the Americans on their own ground (the US was as open to Canadian farm equipment as Canada was to American, so Canadian and American firms did compete on an equal footing throughout the continent).

In this unprotected environment, the Canadian Massey-Harris firm thrived and grew to become today, as Massey-Ferguson, a billion dollar "international corporation" meeting and matching the Americans in every part of the globe. (Massey-Ferguson hasn't been doing too well the past two or three years, but most of the other farm equipment giants have been having their troubles, too; the farmers, it seems, have temporarily stopped buying.)

The Versatile Manufacturing Company of Winnipeg is another illuminating example from the same unprotected industry. Massey-Ferguson demonstrates that Canadians can successfully operate a gigantic, international, multi-product corporation. The people at Versatile demonstrate that imagination, technical ingenuity, hard work and a willingness to take risks are also traits in which Canadians can match Americans if they are given the chance. Versatile is a comparatively tiny firm which has snatched a profitable portion of the farm equipment business away from the giants by developing new products the farmers liked and wanted. More than half of Versatile's sales are in the US.

Massey and Versatile suggest what Canadian industry might have been like if Canadians had not voted enthusiastically for Macdonald's "national policy" in 1878. Fewer, but much larger, Canadian factories would have competed with the international giants on world markets. More industrial research would have been undertaken in Canada and more new products would have been developed here. Ordinary Canadians would have benefitted by paying less for virtually all their manufactured goods. Canadian labour would have been able to bargain with Canadian management — and neither party would have had to conform to instructions from "head office" beyond our borders.

Tariffs, which grew to dizzy heights in the decade of the Great Depression, have been coming down around the world in recent years. But in Canada's case the damage that was done may prove permanent. Our protectionist policies of earlier years have produced the Canadian "branch plant economy" of today and it will not be easy for us to change our status as a tiny, inefficient replica of the American pattern.

Particularly because of the psychological damage that has been done to Canadians. We have come to believe the great lie — that we need American capital to keep Canada's economy growing. And we have come to believe a host of lesser lies, too — that Canadians are not as successfully competitive as Americans; that Canadian businessmen don't know how to hustle; that only the Americans can do effective industrial research and develop new products and techniques; that only Americans know how to manage large and complex business enterprises.

We have, in short, acquired a deepseated sense of inferiority over the years of living in the branch plant economy. We lack faith in our own capabilities — and we hold the Americans in almost reverential awe.

It is perhaps for this reason that the members of our economic elite have been so quick to sell out. Better take our fast buck now than have to hang in there and compete with those Americans; they'd beat us anyway in the end.

And if we have money to lend or invest, better let the Americans handle it; that way we'll be sure to make a profit. Back Canadian ventures and we're likely to lose our shirts.

These attitudes are all too common along Bay Street and St. James Street. Financial houses fall all over each other trying to be the first to provide the capital for a new American-owned venture in Canada. But the same people don't even give the time of day to Canadians with a new idea, or a new enterprise.

It is difficult to believe that powerful and seemingly responsible Canadian financial men think this way, but they do. It is even more difficult to believe that they not only downgrade Canadian competence but seem to exhibit active contempt and repugnance in the one area of innovation, enterprise and wealth-producing creativity in which the Canadians are the world's leaders, but they do.

The story of Canadian mining is a proud record of achievement — and a tragic tale of sabotage and betrayal.

The next chapter is about the incredible industry that could have made Canada rich.

THE INCREDIBLE INDUSTRY

Murray Watts, one of Canada's most energetic and creative mining developers, tells a story.

He was speaking one day to members of the Toronto Stock Exchange when he happened to mention Cobalt. Cobalt? One of the men he was talking to got up to look at a map since, apparently, none of them knew where the place was.

Cobalt!

In 1903, northern Ontario blacksmith Fred LaRose threw his hammer at what he thought were the glowing eyes of a fox but discovered, instead, that he had hit a chunk of shining ore. LaRose knew enough about minerals to know that he needed some expert advice. First, he staked his claims. Then, having established his claims, he spaded out samples of the ore he had found and took them to Haileybury. Fred LaRose's samples eventually reached Dr. W.G. Miller, a geologist at Queen's University.

What Miller saw made him pack his bags and head north. He looked around the staked land and found "pieces of native silver as big as stove lids or cannon balls lying on the ground, as well as cobalt bloom and niccolite".

Meanwhile, Fred LaRose wanted a holiday so he sold half his claims for fifteen hundred dollars and boarded the train for Hull, across the river from Ottawa.

Along the way, he stopped in Mattawa and dropped into Noah Timmins' general store. Noah and his brother Henry were interested in mining. They had often grubstaked prospectors and had even gone out to do a little prospecting themselves.

LaRose showed Noah Timmins samples of the ore he had found, but Noah pretended indifference. As soon as LaRose left, however, Noah telegraphed his brother Henry, who was in Montreal at the time, and told him to hurry to Hull, find LaRose and make a deal with him.

Henry Timmins paid thirty-five hundred dollars for half of LaRose's remaining share of his discovery. LaRose was now $5,000 ahead.

Shortly afterwards there were disputes over LaRose's title to his claims, but he was eventually established as the first finder. The Timmins brothers, having gathered a syndicate around them, now paid LaRose a further $25,000 for his remaining interest in the discovery.

A shaft was sunk but there was no sign of ore below ground. The syndicate might have quit then and there and written off their losses, except that Dr. Miller, the Queen's geologist who had first seen LaRose's samples, convinced them to drive the shaft deeper.

About a hundred feet down they found a rich vein of high quality silver.

The Timmins syndicate sold the LaRose mine for a million dollars. The buyers, before the mine was closed, produced eight million dollars worth of silver.

And Cobalt, the town the Bay Street brokers couldn't find, became one of the great mining boom towns of history, grew to a population of 30,000, and produced three hundred million dollars worth of metal.

Like so many other Canadian mining communities, Cobalt was left with nothing when the mines ran out. Ontario took millions in tax revenue out of the Cobalt mining camp, but put nothing back in the way of permanent development. As a result, Cobalt is now nearly a ghost town, its population down to two thousand and its future dim.

But Cobalt was the first of many spectacular Ontario mining developments. And the LaRose mine gave the Timmins brothers their first taste of the rewards that awaited venturesome and intelligent speculators in Canadian mining.

Cobalt began its slow death after 1907, but the Timmins family didn't lose their interest in Canada's natural resources.

In 1909, the scene of the action had moved to Porcupine Lake, where rich veins of gold were turning up.

A young barber from Haileybury, Benny Hollinger, using a forty-five dollar grub stake provided by Jack McMahon (a bartender) staked the land around a small, abandoned open pit mine. Hollinger and his partner Alex Gillies (who had a grub stake of a hundred dollars) took samples from the bottom of the abandoned pit and had sent them out for assay. The samples contained fifty-two dollars worth of gold. The young men staked their claims around the pit and began to investigate a little more carefully.

Gillies described what happened next*:

Benny was pulling moss off the rocks a few feet away when he suddenly let a roar out of him, and threw his hat to me. At first I thought he was crazy, but when I came over to where he was, it was not hard to find the reason. The quartz where he had taken off the moss looked as though someone had dripped a candle along it, but instead of wax it was gold. The quartz stood up about three feet out of the ground and was about six feet wide, with gold all spattered over it, and for about sixty feet along the vein.

Noah Timmins, who had picked up a million dollars in Cobalt, offered Hollinger and Gillies three hundred and thirty thousand dollars for their claims. This was a brave, perhaps even reckless, act. Noah Timmins had been blooded but he was far from being a scientific mining man; he was playing

*George Lonn, *The Mine Finders,* Pitt Publishing Co., Toronto, 1966.

hunches — and gold mining in Ontario had not, until then, been a particularly profitable activity. As D.M. Lebourdais said, "There were times when all Noah's determination was needed to keep things going."

But keep things going he did, and the Hollinger mine became the second biggest producer of gold in Canada. Noah Timmins also developed the townsite that bears his name. Timmins, Ontario, was created in 1912 to be the commercial and residential centre of the Porcupine gold mining country.

In their first forty-five years, the gold mines of the Porcupine produced one billion, two hundred million dollars worth of gold and paid three hundred and sixty million dollars in dividends.

By 1964, the original Hollinger mine had poured its twenty thousandth bar of gold and Timmins was a thriving city of 30,000 people. The gold mines were beginning to run short of profitable ore and the future of the mines — and the community — looked bleak.

In that year, however, Texas Gulf Sulphur made its sensational base metal strike barely beyond Timmins' municipal boundaries, and the town gained a new lease on life.

The gap between Noah Timmins and Texas Gulf Sulphur is more than the gap of a generation or two in time. Timmins was a small town merchant with daring, imagination and a weakness for risking his every penny on one throw of the dice. He knew the Ontario northland was rich beyond the dreams of avarice and he was willing to gamble that he had latched onto the mother lode of those riches. Texas Gulf was another story.

A large, stodgy and unimaginative American company, Texas Gulf had amassed impressive reserves of cash through its near-control over the American market for sulphur. As the shareholders — and some of the younger employees — became restless, Texas Gulf almost reluctantly embarked on an exploration programme intended to find other exploitable minerals to add to the company's cash flow and profits.

In an offhand and absent-minded way, they allowed some young Canadian employees to use the latest scientific techniques for mine-finding to explore selected portions of Canada. A massive capital commitment enabled them to undertake a thorough investigation of all the territory they found interesting. One of the pieces of land they investigated turned out to be solid pay-dirt, and the fabulous Texas Gulf deposits of zinc, lead, copper and silver were proved up.

The Texas Gulf discoveries near Timmins produced a flurry of interest in Canadian mining stocks. Earlier in the century each new mining discovery generated a stock market boom as speculative companies staked claims in the areas surrounding the latest discovery. Millions of shares a day churned through what was once the Toronto Standard Stock Exchange and through the Toronto Stock Exchange itself. Most of the Johnny-come-lately speculators lost their money; they were less interested in mines than they were in hoping to sell the shares they bought today for fifty cents, to somebody else tomorrow for a dollar. But, prior to the Texas Gulf discovery, the mining market had financed the highly speculative, high risk mining exploration business with a considerable degree of success. The "Windfall Scandal" which followed the Texas Gulf discoveries marked, however, a benchmark in the Canadian resources exploration industry. Viola Macmillan, once president of the Prospectors and Developers Association, was convicted for her role in the promotion and manipulation of Windfall Oils and Mines.

With Mrs. Macmillan's conviction, the Toronto investment community breathed a sigh of satisfaction. The law was — at last! — catching up with the bandits who dominated the Canadian mining business.

But the sad truth is that Viola Macmillan's behaviour was no more — and perhaps a lot less — reprehensible than the behaviour of a thousand and one other speculators who had pushed Canada to world preeminence in mining development. And it certainly didn't involve any larger investor risks, nor result in any larger investor losses than the market performance of a great many "junior industrials" underwritten and distributed by some of the Toronto Stock Exchange's most respectable member houses.

A glance at the recent performance figures of some of the non-mining securities traded on the Toronto Stock Exchange makes the point:

Name of Company	1969 High	1970 Low	% Decline
Cap. Diversified Ind.	$ 8.88	$0.75	91.6
Computel Systems	45.00	3.25	92.8
Comtech Group	19.00	1.00	94.7
Dylex Diversified	40.25	3.75	90.7
Harvey's Foods	12.50	.57	95.4
Invest. Overseas Mgmt.	71.50	3.80	94.7
OSF Industries	34.50	2.50	92.8
Riley's Datashare	20.00	1.00	95.5
Toromont Industries	4.30	.40	90.7
Van-Ness Industries	9.75	.40	96.0

In spite of figures like these, the impression remains that buying speculative mining shares is almost as risky as buying lottery tickets while buying "industrial" shares is almost as safe as putting your money in the mattress.

Because of the genuine — as opposed to the manipulated — risks involved, mining speculation has always been a chancy thing, both for the promoter and for the investing public. The chances of finding a mine — even in this scientific age — are necessarily so slim that no sane man would invest if he had the probabilities explained to him. So the promoter paints the brightest picture he can — if he didn't, he wouldn't attract the risk capital, and if he can't attract the capital, he can't afford to drill a single hole — and he also tries to minimize the risks by aiming to test and explore as many properties as he can, more or less at the same time; if there isn't an ore body on one set of claims, there may be on another!

Up and down the line in Texas Gulf Sulphur, it appears that officers, executives and employees took advantage of their inside positions to make enormous profits on their knowledge of the company's startling mineral strike at Kidd Creek near Timmins. None of them, so far, has gone to jail.

But Mrs. Macmillan became the scapegoat — for doing what Canadian mining developers and stock brokers have always done, for encouraging risk takers to participate in the most exciting risk of all, the search for mineral wealth.

Viola Macmillan had been in conflict with, and a vocal critic of, the rules and regulations of the Toronto Stock Exchange for years, but she had also been a successful promoter and developer of producing mines and had become a prominent spokesman for the neglected interests of mining and the mining men in her position as president of the Prospectors and Developers Association. A multitude of other speculative mining ventures had financial and trading histories similar to Mrs. Macmillan's Windfall. And the largest of the "industrial mines" were traditionally just as secretive about the results of exploration as she had been with her Windfall results.

It is very difficult indeed not to conclude that Mrs. Macmillan was singled out for punishment because of her courageous criticism of the Toronto financial community, the Toronto Stock Exchange and the legislators and regulatory bodies who, theoretically, controlled the behaviour of Toronto's markets.

The "Windfall Scandal" went a long way towards completing a smear campaign against Canada's broker-dealers and promoters. The old Standard Stock Exchange, which had played such an important role in the development of Canada's most important mines, was long gone, absorbed by the

Toronto Stock Exchange in the 1930's.

And a new group — the members of the economic elite — had moved in on the Toronto Stock Exchange. The men who control the wealth in Canada realized that the operations of the Stock Exchange were a further source of wealth and power. The old, established investment houses which had built fortunes in the respectable, but highly profitable business of dealing in bonds and government securities became very interested in the business of trading in equities on behalf of the public.

When these men moved in on the Canadian stock market they didn't like the way the game was being played, so, using their financial and political power, they changed the rules.

A new kind of respectability, we were told, was being brought to the Toronto Stock Exchange. Never again would the public be taken for suckers by fast-talking mining promoters pushing acres of moose pasture. We have seen, in the table above, just how "secure" securities can be in the new-style, highly regulated stock market. How well the investment dealers, their private club, the Toronto Stock Exchange, and their tame regulatory agency, the Ontario Securities Commission, together with their friends in New York, have lived up to their implied promises of a fair shake for the investor in an honest market we will see in the next chapter.

But before we leave the mining industry, we must pay tribute to the men who built it by glancing briefly at what they built. In 1963, Canada's mineral production (including fossil fuels) was valued at $3 billion. Minerals accounted for about one third of our total merchandise exports which were valued at $6,800,000,000. We were first in the world in nickel, second in gold, third in iron and zinc, fourth in silver and lead, and fifth in copper. In nickel, we accounted for fully 80% of the non-Communist world's total supply of this vital metal.

Altogether an impressive contribution to the world's

resources from a nation inhabited by fewer than one percent of the world's people.

Of course, two thirds of our mining and three quarters of our fossil fuel industries are owned by foreigners.

WALL STREET:
THE GREATEST CASINO

At the beginning of this century, Canadians sensed that their inheritance of natural resources could make them as rich as Croesus.

The name of Canada was magic throughout the world from the days of the Klondike Gold Rush until the early fifties. Canada's incredible bounty and limitless future prosperity were reflected in the stock exchanges. In 1954, you could buy a seat on the New York Stock Exchange for $80,000, but a seat on the Toronto Stock Exchange was worth $140,000. The volume of trading on the NYSE was below three million shares a day. In Toronto the daily turnover of shares ran at around four million.

But Wall Street was fighting — successfully as it turned out — for its life.

By early 1971, trading on the TSE averaged less than three million shares — down twenty-five percent in a decade and a half — while the NYSE was churning over twenty million shares a day — up almost 700 percent.

The 1968 value of a seat on the Toronto Exchange was down to $80,000, while seats on the New York Stock Exchange changed hands for as much as $550,000.

New York, members of the Canadian investment community believed, was where the action was. The financial section of the Canadian economic elite had simply lost interest in Canada and its future.

A dryly titled report, *The Supply of, and Demand for, Canadian Equities,* "A study commissioned from the Faculty of Administrative Studies, York University, Toronto, by the Toronto Stock Exchange and prepared by Professor G.R. Conway", reveals in massive and depressing detail the pattern of ownership of equity in Canadian companies.*

"It is not the function of this study," the Conway Report says, "to discuss the policy implications of substantial amounts of the savings of Canadians flowing directly and indirectly into the equity securities of foreign corporations." In spite of this disclaimer, the facts presented in the Report sketch the outline of an almost totally incredible picture. Here are a few of those facts:

"About 30% in value of the total trading in the 101 (largest Canadian) companies takes place on United States stock exchanges."

"The turnover of Canadian stocks on the Toronto Stock Exchange is substantially less than the New York Exchange figure."

"While the Canadian (life insurance) companies have only 4% of their Canadian assets in stocks, they have 10% of their foreign assets invested in stocks (a proportion that even exceeds the 6% of the United States companies)."

"Canadian financial institutions (pension funds, mutual funds, insurance companies) held only 10% of their stock portfolio in foreign stocks in 1960, but the proportion had grown to 24% by the end of 1966 . . . the open end investment funds (mutual funds) have the largest holdings of foreign stocks, with over 35% of their stock portfolio in foreign

*Conway, a brilliant young economist, was one of Walter Gordon's famous "whiz kids", a trio of thinkers who joined Mr. Gordon's staff in Ottawa when he became Finance Minister. The "whiz kids" became a political *cause célèbre* when it was discovered that they were involved in preparation of the budget and privy to budget secrets although they were not regular civil servants. It is entirely possible that the "whiz kids" became an issue not because of their lack of civil service status, but because they shared Mr. Gordon's conviction that drastic steps needed to be taken to restore to Canadians economic control of their country.

securities at the end of 1966 (a proportion that had increased to 53% by the end of 1967)."

Can it be true? Can it be that more shares in Canada's largest companies are bought and sold in New York than in Canada?

Can it be that, while Canadian politicians, economists and investment dealers are telling us we need more and more foreign capital, our mutual funds have put more than half of the money we have invested with them into U.S. stocks?

It isn't as though there were a surplus of innovative risk capital in Canada. Ralph Hedlin, president of the Winnipeg consulting firm, Hedlin, Menzies and Associates Limited, has said, "There are a great many ideas that are not converted into investment, jobs and income because the individuals cannot get the necessary seed capital. There are a great many potential entrepreneurs who could combine capital and labour and show a profit but cannot get the necessary start-up capital."*

Thus, while our professional money managers have been gathering up Canadian wealth and shipping it off by the bushel to New York, new and innovative Canadian enterprises have been starved for capital.

It can, of course, be argued that the money goes to New York because there's a higher return for lower risk in American securities. It can be argued — but it can't be argued successfully. The NYSE is the world's greatest casino and, as in every other casino, only the house wins in the long run; the players are eventually separated from their money. To provide just a fraction of the total picture, the table opposite depicts the stock market performance of the shares of seventeen large and well-known American companies during the past few years.

While the public was losing $61 billion in the common

*"Risk Capital and Human Development." by Ralph Hedlin, in *Living in the Seventies*, Peter Martin Associates, Toronto, 1970.

RISK IN U.S. STOCKS

Company	No. Shs. Issued	High 1964 or Later	Price June 30, 1970	Dollar Decline	% Decline
Amer. Tel & Tel	541,000,000	75	41 1/4	17,158,750,000	45.0
Boeing	21,612,000	112 3/8	12 1/2	1,891,050,000	88.8
Chrysler	47,360,000	72 3/4	18	2,572,685,000	74.9
du Pont	46,439,000	261	113 7/8	6,785,753,000	56.0
Eastern Airlines	11,957,000	61 5/8	12 7/8	582,904,000	79.1
Freeport Sulfur	15,496,000	78	14 3/8	985,933,000	81.5
General Dynamics	10,570,000	79	17 1/8	654,019,000	78.3
General Motors	287,567,000	113 3/4	62 1/8	15,133,213,000	46.3
Getty Oil	19,985,000	110 1/4	43	1,341,991,000	60.9
Gulf & Western	16,426,000	66 1/8	12 3/8	882,897,000	81.3
Ling Temco Vought	4,669,000	169 1/2	12 3/4	731,866,000	92.5
Litton Ind.	25,503,000	120 3/8	15 3/4	2,668,251,000	86.9
Monsanto Chemical	133,014,000	95	30 1/8	2,141,783,000	68.3
Occidental Pete	49,352,000	55 3/8	24 1/2	2,029,601,000	74.2
Pan American	34,328,000	39 5/8	8 3/4	1,059,927,000	77.9
Penn Central	24,085,000	86 1/2	6 3/4	1,872,609,000	89.8
Union Carbide	60,455,000	75 7/8	33 7/8	2,538,110,000	55.3
Total of dollar decline				61,031,342,000	

shares of these seventeen companies, a further $9 billion or so was being sliced off the value of the same companies' bonds.

An American observer of the Wall Street scene puts it very explicitly in his bestselling book, *The Wall Street Jungle*.* Richard Ney says:

> Much that is painful in our society is due to the public's belief in the cant of the Exchange's chief organs of opinion. Indeed, hidden behind a facade of pompous jargon and noble affectations, there is more sheer larceny per square foot on the floor of the New York Stock Exchange than any place else in the world. It is the legacy of a communal effort that has become a property right, handed down from father to son to grandson. It is sustained by the exclusive allegiance of its high priests to a tradition that wars against reason and that has become so powerful that anyone setting himself against it on behalf of a higher loyalty soon finds he has set himself against a power that is identical to that of government itself.
>
> Clearly, the lunatic economics of this larceny appeal to the criminal. The story is told that after he had been deported to Italy, Lucky Luciano granted an interview in which he described a visit to the floor of the New York Stock Exchange. When the operations of floor specialists had been explained to him, he said, "A terrible thing happened. I realized I'd joined the wrong mob!"

Or, again, Ney's succinct summary:

> The New York Stock Exchange tries to present itself as having a highly moral code. From my vantage point, it would seem that the Exchange's rituals have more to do with providing a casino-like facility for gambling than anything else — and the tables are rigged.

The remarkable rise and fall of the New York market in

*The Wall Street Jungle, by Richard Ney, Grove Press, New York, 1970.

the past few years has been attributed to an American innovation in investment theory — the "performance cult", an idea embraced with enthusiasm by New York money managers: jump in and out of stocks fast, look for quick, short term growth, forget about the fundamental values that the shares of a company might have, just get "performance".

Although he does not speak with the rashness of a Richard Ney, the distinguished American investment analyst David L. Babson, had this to say about the "performance cult" in a *Financial Post* interview late in 1970:

> It fostered abuses, improprieties, unsavory actions, and unethical practices from which many a leader in the investment community grew fat and rich. It paid more people more money for contributing less to society than any group has ever been paid before. And it lost more money for more people than any other get-rich-quick fad in history. From almost any point of view, the Performance Era of the late 1960's will go down as one of the sorriest periods in all financial annals.

If this is what New York is like — a gigantic casino with blatantly rigged tables, a gambling hall where the house always wins — why would Canadian investment funds flow southward?

The simple and superficially acceptable answer as set forth very clearly in the Conway study is that there simply aren't enough investment opportunities available in Canada. On a very conservative projection, the Conway Report indicates that Canadian institutions and individuals will have about $1,300 million available each year for the next eight years to invest in common stocks. But, because of the deficiencies and distortions of the Canadian investment community, new issues of shares can be expected to total only about $700 million a year. Thus, the Report observes, unless circumstances change, "the acquisition of foreign stocks by Canadians will increase dramatically."

There is a kind of madness in this. From coast to coast in Canada, politicians and businessmen on the chicken-and-peas luncheon circuit tell us again and again that we must have foreign capital if we are to develop our economy. And while the speeches are being made Canadian risk capital — the money that should be invested in Canadian ventures — flows south in the millions every day. Simultaneously, incredibly, the Americans continue to take over Canadian companies; in 1968 at least 154 Canadian businesses passed into foreign hands.

The Canadian financial institutions (pension funds, mutual funds, insurance companies) are heavy investors in US securities, sending abroad funds that are badly needed for Canadian development. Because these same institutions are the usual vehicle for stock market participation by all but the wealthy, "a substantial proportion of the savings of low and middle income Canadians would be indirectly invested in non-Canadian industry," says the Conway Report.

Canadian investment dollars flow south partly because the Canadian investment community does not supply enough new stock offerings in Canada to meet the demand.

And one of the major reasons there aren't enough new stock offerings in Canada is that a very large percentage of Canadian industry is in the hands of private companies which do not offer shares to the public.

In 1964 there were approximately 127,000 active corporations in Canada. But 500 of these — less than half of one per cent — accounted for 45% of the assets, over 50% of the profits and over 60% of the dividends of all non-financial corporations (in oil and mining, they accounted for over 60% of total assets).

Of these large and powerful corporations, 43% did not have an issue of publicly traded stock. And of these private companies, almost 80% were controlled by non-residents.

While Canadian money was flowing into — and being lost

on — Wall Street, Canadians were unable to invest in many of the largest and most profitable corporations operating in Canada, because these were private corporations, closely controlled by American and other foreign investors.

And at the same time, because of the structural deficiencies of the Canadian investment community and the narrow and shortsighted perspective of the members of the economic elite who man the Bay Street Temple, Canadian innovators and entrepreneurs were unable to find the "seed capital" necessary to turn good ideas into new industries.

Maurice R. Hecht, writing in the *Globe and Mail*, reports the findings of a US Department of Commerce study undertaken a few years ago on technological innovation. The study found that 80% of important new technological innovations came from "non-incorporated" sources and only 20% from the big industrial research labs. In other words, most of the best new ideas come from people who don't have the money to turn an idea into an industry. The breakthroughs are more likely to come from the guy tinkering in his garage than from the gleaming industrial research facility.

Canada abounds in innovators. A German-Canadian technician near Ottawa comes up with a revolutionary new process for the automated cleaning of movie film. A young Toronto boy develops a prototype fuel cell that generates electricity out of, literally, garbage. A Nova Scotia man designs and builds a lighter, sturdier, cheaper and more comfortable camper-trailer than any on the market. A team of researchers at the University of Toronto comes up with a "degradable" plastic which promises to eliminate the pollution caused by plastics which refuse to decompose when they are thrown away. And so it goes. Every year and in all parts of the country, imaginative and creative Canadians develop new products and processes that might, if encouraged, produce new jobs and new industries for Canada.

But we don't provide the encouragement. Carrying a new

product from the first prototype through to the production line is a time-consuming and expensive process. The inventor rarely has the funds himself to do the job. And, in Canada, he can't find the money anywhere else in the private sector (increasingly, public money — through such agencies as the Industrial Development Bank and the Ontario Development Corporation — has moved into the vacuum, but not yet in adequate amounts).

Our banks behave, in Ralph Hedlin's words, like pawn brokers; they'll lend money against full security, but they won't take risks.

Our investment dealers, as Murray Watts reported, don't know where to find Cobalt without a map. They don't know how to identify a technical innovation, either — and there are no maps on the frontiers of technology.

The Canadian innovator almost invariably has only one of two choices. Either he forgets about his crazy dream and goes back to his honest job. Or, if he's lucky, he sells his product or process to a large corporation which already has the funds to do the development work.

Bill Stroud, wheelchair-bound inventor in McKeller, Ontario, has developed a genuine "breakthrough" kind of printing press. For a dozen years his company has been kept going with the greatest of difficulty but, because of the unavailability of development money, it has never grown as it should have. Unable to find the funds to build presses for sale in the US and elsewhere, the Canadian company has had to license an American company to use its patents. The press is now being built and sold in the US and it is the talk of the printing trade. Although in Canada the machine is known, appropriately and correctly, as the Stroud press, in the US it is becoming famous as the Cameron Press, so named after the American company that is exploiting Bill Stroud's patents.

The depressing story can be told over and over again in our natural resource industries as well. Oil men and mining developers knock in vain on Bay Street doors, and finally are forced to accept American money – and American control – to turn a discovery into a producing property.

While the little people with the ideas can't find the money they need, the big companies that dominate Canada's economy are able, by and large, to finance their further growth without outside money.

Professor John Warnock of the University of Saskatchewan recently called attention, in the *Toronto Star,* to the most recent (1968) figures on "Sources of New US direct Investment in Canada", which have been released by the US Department of Commerce. The figures presented by Professor Warnock look like this:

	US millions
Total New US Direct Investment in Canada	3,611
sources	
Retained earnings	1,027
Depreciation and Depletion	864
Funds from Abroad	539
Other Sources and adjustments	53
New Funds from the U.S.	127

"New funds from the US" accounted for $127 million out of $3,611 million total new US investment in Canada. That's *less than 5%.* The largest source of the funds producing the rapid growth of US ownership of our economy was the money generated by the US companies already operating here. Retained earnings and depreciation and depletion allowances provided more than half of the growth of US investment in Canada. And both those items, without argument or qualification, represent Made in Canada dollars.

Professor Warnock also brings the balance of accounts up to date. In 1968, the Americans took out of Canada, on balance, $487 million. In 1969 they took out $511 million.

The figures can be expected to continue to rise. And they are *net* figures — the dollars the Americans have put into Canada have been subtracted from the dollars they have taken out, and the net balance shows them taking over a billion dollars out of Canada in the past two years.

We, of course, were adding to the net outflow of funds by sending our money off to Wall Street.

Clearly the Canadian economy would grow faster if Canadian savings were invested in Canada. A higher rate of local capital investment would produce a more vigourous economy. And a more vigorous economy would generate a multitude of benefits — not least of which would be a dramatic reduction in unemployment. With lower unemployment, less public money would be spent on unemployment insurance benefits and other social welfare transfer payments. On the positive side, full employment would swell the government's coffers because more people would be earning taxable incomes and paying more taxes.

Unfortunately, it isn't possible to bring this Utopia to pass simply by waving a magic wand. We have sold too large a portion of our economy to recover control of it immediately; too many Canadians — especially those with economic and, indirectly, political power — are too satisfied with things as they are to change their minds over night; and, ultimately, the American government in Washington has too much potential power to exert economic pressure upon us; for all these reasons any programme to regain control of our own destiny must be carefully planned and carefully executed.

But it *is* possible. We *can* do it. We can take Canada back for the Canadians. Not easily, and perhaps not quickly, but certainly.

YOUR FIFTY-FIVE
THOUSAND DOLLARS

Carl O. Nickle is publisher of *Daily Oil Bulletin,* the highly successful, Calgary-based newsletter that keeps everybody who's interested right on top of developments in our petroleum industry. Mr. Nickle is as impartial and as expert a commentator on the industry as you'll find in this country. And he's the man who added up all the figures last year and came to the incredible conclusion that Canada's petroleum resources are worth at least fifty-five thousand dollars for every man, woman and child in this country.

Writing in *Canadian Petroleum* in May, 1970, Mr. Nickle explained it this way:

A few months ago the Canadian Petroleum Association completed a detailed appraisal of all pertinent government and industry data, and came up with careful, conservative calculations of Canada's hydrocarbon potential. In brief, potential for conventional liquid petroleums was placed at over 140 billion barrels — 45 billion in Western Canada, 43 billion in the Arctic, 25 billion in the Atlantic region, and lesser volumes elsewhere. Natural gas potential was put at 725 trillion cubic feet, with the West and Arctic dominating. In addition, Alberta's tar sands have a potential of over 300 billion barrels of synthetic oil, while the sands and Alberta gasfields have a potential of over one billion tons of sulphur.

What are these potentials worth? Using deliberately conservative figures, based on today's Western Canadian field prices for oil, gas and sulphur, I calculate that the potential when found and produced will generate a gross revenue in Canada of $1,118 billions . . . .

Opinions will vary from my guesstimates, as to whether they be reasonable, conservative or optimistic. But it should be abundantly clear that Canada, and all of its citizens, have a vital stake in the decisions that must soon be made by government leaders, and the subsequent multiplicity of decisions that will be made by a host of Canadian and foreign investors interested in Canada's natural resources.

Available evidence suggests that Mr. Nickle was being deliberately conservative in his "guesstimates". The Nickle estimate, for example, assumes 43 billion barrels of oil in Canada's Arctic regions, but John Andriuk, an expert with Dome Petroleum, a firm deeply into Arctic oil exploration, places the potential of the Mackenzie Delta and the Arctic islands at 85 billion barrels — almost exactly twice as large a reserve of oil as Mr. Nickle postulates. Again, the estimate by Carl Nickle and the Canadian Petroleum Institute assumes only 25 billion barrels of recoverable oil in the Atlantic region; at the time the estimate was made, the presence of *any* signif- icant quantities of oil off our east coast was a matter of speculation, but early in the summer of 1971 there was an oil strike on Sable Island of sufficient importance, or so the press reported, to bring tears to the eyes of Premier Regan of Nova Scotia. And, yet again, an article by David S. Boyer in *National Geographic Magazine* in 1968 places the oil potential of the Athabaska tar sands not at Mr. Nickle's 300 billion barrels, but at twice that much: "The black, sticky tar sands lie in sedimentary beds up to 200 feet thick, spread across an incredible 30,000 square miles. They contain an estimated 600 billion barrels of oil — twice the known oil reserves of all the rest of the non-Communist world."

The most cautious feature of Mr. Nickle's valuation, however, is that he was deriving his figures from "field" or well-head prices at 1970 levels. He made no allowance for the fact that the world's — and in particular, the United States' — insatiable appetite for petroleum products is almost certain to drive prices up, both absolutely and relatively, before Canada's potential is fully exploited. Nor did he build into his calculations the value added by transportation, processing and transformation of petroleum between the time it surges to the surface of the earth and the time it serves the consumer, powering his car, heating his house, or forming the raw material of the pharmaceuticals that keep him healthy or the plastics that embellish his life. A generally accepted yardstick multiplies the "field" price of petroleum by a factor of five by the time it reaches the consumer.

Carl O. Nickle says our petroleum resources are worth slightly more than $1.1 trillion, or about $55,000 for every person alive in Canada today. If we assume continuing steady inflation, we can double that figure. And if we assume that Canadians are selling not crude oil at well-head, but sophisticated end-products of the petro-chemical industry, then we can multiply the figure again by a factor of five.

Which means our petroleum resources could be worth somewhat more than ten trillion dollars — or about a half-million dollars for every Canadian.

You say you've got a wife and three kids? So your family's share of our nation's petro-chemical potential comes to about two and a half million dollars.

Of course, you never get something for nothing. Enormous sums have to be invested in exploration to find the oil, in pipelines to move it from there to here, in refineries, in factories, in service stations and in pure, egg-head research to get the greatest value out of the complex hydrocarbon molecules that a billion years of activity of life and near-life on Space Ship Earth have bequeathed to us.

So let's, for the moment, forget all the multipliers. Let's just deal with Carl O. Nickle's basic figure of $1,118 billion as the value of our oil reserves. Just $55,000 for every Canadian.

Too bad we won't get it.

In 1963 our petroleum industry was 74% foreign controlled, 64% foreign owned and the percentages have risen since then.

Our petroleum refineries are more than 99% foreign controlled.

It wasn't always thus.

The Canadian oil industry, surprisingly, started in Ontario. James M. Williams dug our first oil well at Oil Springs in southwestern Ontario in 1857 (two years before the discovery at Titusville, Pennsylvania, that gave the American oil industry its start). Mr. Williams built our first refinery to turn his crude oil into kerosene for lamps. In 1860, a richer oil discovery was made at Petrolia, Ontario. Prospectors rushed to the area and production climbed steadily until it reached 800,000 barrels a day in 1895. Today a bare trickle of oil comes from the once-rich fields, but the economic benefits have lasted; nearby Sarnia is a major centre for Canada's chemical industry and headquarters for the highly successful, government-owned Polymer Corporation.

The increase in production in the Petrolia area and the development of the competitive Pennsylvania fields led to a dramatic reduction in the cost of kerosene. In 1859, Canadians paid a dollar a gallon for their "coal oil", but by 1880 the price had fallen to 12¢. During the same period, Canada became an exporter of petroleum products. Local demand could not absorb all the oil coming from the new wells and refineries, so more than half of Canadian production was being exported to Europe by the mid-1870's.

Intense competition and the drop in prices forced several of the principal Canadian producers to amalgamate. In 1880, they organized Imperial Oil Limited. In 1889 the fledgling company moved its refinery from Petrolia to Sarnia — and sold a majority of its voting stock to Rockefeller's Standard

Oil Company in order to raise the money to build the new Sarnia refinery. Imperial Oil has since grown to have the largest sales of any company in Canada.

James Laxer, in *The Energy Poker Game* , makes these comments on today's Imperial Oil:

Typically, people think of a company like Imperial Oil simply as a large company in the oil business. The truth is that Imperial is like a feudal fiefdom. It is held from above by the majestic giant of multi-national corporations, Jersey Standard. But below are its own subsidiaries.

Laxer then presents a list of no fewer than thirty active Canadian companies, owned and controlled by Imperial.

In 1970 the company's sales were $1,680,000,000. Imperial Oil had net, after tax, earnings of $105,000,000. It has paid a dividend every year since 1900.

But that's not the whole story. A little simple arithmetic produces figures for Imperial's assets that move the company's image from the gigantic to the totally incredible.

Although there is no conventional reason to question the contents of Imperial Oil's financial statements, prepared, as the auditors say, "according to generally accepted accounting principles", the balance sheet, with its $1,555,000,000 in assets simply doesn't reflect the real financial strength of the company. Commonly accepted estimates placed Canada's proven petroleum reserves at around $50 billion. And, of this $50 billion in proven reserves, outside industry estimates place Imperial's share at around 30% (Imperial itself is less than explicit about its reserves). Thus Imperial Oil's real assets (not fully shown on the balance sheet) can be guesstimated at $15 billion — ten times the stated figure.

With Jersey Standard owning just about 70% of Imperial, can see that the American parent can comfortably claim ownership of something like $10.5 billion worth of Canada's wealth.

But that's only the beginning. Continuing exploration will, in Carl Nickle's estimate, raise Canada's total petroleum wealth to that $1.1 trillion figure quoted at the beginning of this chapter. Imperial, like the other multinational, integrated petroleum giants, has an aggressive exploration programme built into its corporate objectives. Imperial is exploring off Canada's Atlantic coast as well as in the Arctic: (But it was a Mobil discovery well that brought tears to the eye of Premier Regan — and howls of anguish from conservationists who feared oil exploitation would destroy the unique ecology of Sable Island), so there can be little doubt that the company will maintain its share-of-market as additional reserves are proven. And 30% of $1.1 trillion is, of course, $333 billion. Of this remarkable sum of money, Jersey Standard's share, based on the present distribution of ownership of Imperial, will amount to a far from trivial $233 billion.

Pierre Elliot Trudeau was born with the proverbial silver spoon in his mouth and he is — and will remain — independently wealthy. This may help explain something about the man's attitude towards public service: rich men don't *need* to be Prime Minister. And it's just possible that the source of his wealth may explain a lot about his ambiguous and ambivalent attitude towards the foreign takeover of the Canadian economy.

The Trudeau family fortune was built in the oil business. Pierre Elliot's father was a founder of the Automobile Owners' Association, an organization which served its members, in part, by retailing petroleum products. In the 1930's the gas retailing organization became Champlain Oil and a subsidiary of Imperial Oil. Trudeau *père* reportedly came out of the transfer of ownership with $1.4 million dollars; the money, subsequently invested shrewdly in real estate and other ventures, eventually made our present Prime Minister an independently wealthy man.

Imperial is the largest of the foreign-controlled petroleum

giants actively exploiting Canada's resources, but the others are not too far behind. And their histories are depressingly parallel to that of Imperial. From tiny, speculative, Canadian-owned corporations, they have become carefully-controlled subsidiaries of the multinational giants.

In 1901, Canadian Oil Companies Limited was organized in Petrolia. Canadian Oil — whose White Rose trademark was familiar to Canadian motorists until 1962 — was taken over by the British-Dutch giant, Shell Oil, in that year for about $150 million. By 1970 Shell Canada had stated assets of $957,989,000.

In 1907, the first refinery of the British-American Oil Company was opened in Toronto. The sign of "The Big B-A" was also familiar to Canadians until the end of 1968. On January 1st, 1969, the company changed its name from the British-American Oil Company Limited to Gulf Oil Canada Limited. The old signs came down and new ones went up. Wayne and Shuster donned running shoes and covorted on the TV screen to make Canadians comfortable with the new corporate image and trademark. The company's total assets at December 31, 1968, were $921,998,000. Shareholders equity at the same date was $650,607,000. Gulf Oil Corporation of Pittsburgh holds 69% of outstanding common shares. The name change in 1969 was only a matter of tidying up. Gulf had taken control of B-A thirteen years earlier, in 1956.

Remember McColl-Frontenac? In 1925 Frontenac Oil Refineries Ltd. was formed in Montreal, later amalgamating with McColl Brothers Limited, a producer of lubricants which had been in business since 1873. McColl-Frontenac became Texaco Canada Limited in February, 1959, after an exchange of shares. Texaco Canada Limited has assets of $328,602,000, and shareholder equity of $170,410,000. Texaco International Financial Corporation holds 68.1% of the common, voting shares of Texaco Canada. Texaco International Financial is a wholly-owned subsidiary of Texaco Inc.

Pacific Petroleums Ltd. was incorporated in British Columbia in 1939. In 1960, Pacific traded almost six million of its shares for the Canadian assets of Phillips Petroleum Company. At the end of 1969, Phillips Petroleum International Investment Company of Bartlesville, Oklahoma, held 48% of Pacific's outstanding shares. Pacific has assets (end of 1968) of $403,674,000. It is, of course, controlled by Phillips. Pacific, in turn, holds a controlling 22% interest in Westcoast Transmission, a pipeline and gas marketing organization with assets of $373,44,000.

It isn't just the big Canadian companies that have fallen under the control of foreign interests, but the smaller ones as well, especially the smaller ones with growth potential. In fact, the mechanics of the foreign takeover of Canada's natural resources can best be seen in the case histories of some of the smaller energy-oriented companies.

Banff Oil Limited, for example. A Canadian company organized in 1951, Banff was engaged in exploration for and development of crude oil, natural gas and related products in western and northern Canada. Banff's early history was unexceptional but the company was well-managed in a business where even good management didn't ensure success. Banff's stock traded as low as 92¢ in 1963 and even in 1965 the low was $1.30. But Banff's activities had attracted the attention of Aquitaine Company of Canada Limited, a much larger and better financed operation. Aquitaine was owned 82.4% by SNPA (Société National des Petroles d'Aquitaine), a creature of the French government, which directly owns 51% of SNPA.

In 1964 Aquitaine made a public tender offer for 1,400,000 outstanding Banff shares — just under 40% of the company — with Lehman Brothers in New York and Greenshields Inc. of Montreal acting as financial agents. Aquitaine offered $2.50 a share at a time when Banff was trading at $2.30, and the offer was oversubscribed. Banff fell under the control of Aquitaine. J.C. Rudolph, president of Banff Oil, had publicly expressed his bitterness at the Canadian investment community's lack of enthusiasm for investment in oil exploration but, unable to raise sufficient money through the Canadian investment community, he had gone along with the Aquitaine arrangement (by 1967, three years later, he had mellowed somewhat, at least in his public statements. Canadians, he said then, just didn't have the money for risk ventures. "They are still at the life-insurance buying stage," he said.)

This trivial takeover of a small and not very successful Canadian exploration company by a European firm that didn't have its name on any North American gas stations might not have been of much interest to anyone — except that Banff Oil brought in the rich Rainbow Lake oil field in northern Alberta in 1965.

In the Rainbow Lake venture, Socony-Mobil had a 50% interest, Aquitaine a 45% interest, and Banff — which actually did the work — a 5% interest. Rainbow was a bonanza; the president of Imperial Oil (a competitor) called it the greatest discovery since Leduc. Banff shares rose, hitting highs of $9.85 in 1965, $18.37 in 1967 and $19.75 in 1969. Aquitaine, of course, had paid $2.50 each for almost a million and a half of these shares, so the French government was enjoying a capital gain that might have stayed in Canadian hands if Toronto's investment community had been as willing to take a risk on Banff's ability to find oil as Aquitaine had been (the Canadian financial community maintained its myopia; in November, 1968, Gairdner and Company advised its clients to sell out their Banff shares — they were, the Gairdner people proclaimed, overpriced at $12.75!).

Aquitaine had paid $3,500,000 for its interest in Banff in 1964. At 1969 market prices, this investment was worth a low of about $14,700,000 and a high of close to $28,000,000. In terms of Canada's natural resources, Aquitaine controlled Banff's proved petroleum reserves — at the end of 1968, almost 30 million barrels of crude oil, over four million barrels of natural gas liquids, over 120 billion cubic feet of natural gas and half a million tons of sulphur.

The value of these petroleum products at well-head prices is substantially more than $100 million. The French investors hadn't done badly for themselves. Their $3,500,000 investment had turned into resources worth at least $40 million in the short space of four years.

Acquitaine's impressive profit through direct investment in Banff Oil represents, however, only a tiny fraction of the French company's gains from Banff's discovery of the Rainbow field. Remember that, besides its controlling interest in Banff, Acquitaine also had, separately, a 45% interest in any discoveries Banff made in its Rainbow drilling program. The cost of Banff's discovery well was around $300,000, so Acquitaine's outlay of money amounted to about $135,000.

But Banff's discovery amounted to about 600,000,000 barrels of oil worth, at well-head prices, $1,800,000,000 (just in case you missed a few of the zeroes, that's one billion, eight hundred million dollars). Acquitaine gets 45% of that, or $810,000,000 (eight hundred and ten million dollars).

This neat little windfall lifted Acquitaine into the ranks of the majors in the North American oil business. And it certainly represented a good return on an investment of $135,000.

If John Rudolph of Banff had been able to get adequate financial support from Canadians, then Banff would have joined the front-runners, not Acquitaine. A Canadian firm, not a foreign firm. In the upshot, the Canadian firm vanished.

John Rudolph had wanted to keep Banff Canadian, but the men on Bay Street weren't interested. The Canadian investment dealers and members of the economic elite found much more satisfaction in steering their clients' money to Wall Street.

At the end of 1970, Banff Oil Disappeared — merged into Aquitaine through an exchange of shares, 100 Banff shares for 52 Aquitaine.

The story of Dynamic Petroleum is, if anything, even more illuminating. Dynamic was the keystone of a group of small but high-flying western exploration companies, promoted, controlled and operated by an aggressive team from Calgary.

Dynamic Petroleum Products Limited was established in 1958 as the successor firm to Dynamic Petroleum Limited.

Like so many other speculative, resource-oriented companies, Dynamic was viewed with disfavour on Bay Street. In 1961, the latent tension between the Calgary developers and the conservative members of the Bay Street establishment flared into open conflict. Dynamic president Archie P. Newall sent a letter to his shareholders urging them to buy all the shares they could lay their hands on; the price of Dynamic stock had been dropping and, said Newell, "there is a reasonably large short position in the stock". His clear implication was that the company was being raided. A Bay Street group was selling stock they didn't own (selling short) in an effort to drive prices down so they could buy in later (cover their short positions) at a lower price and reap a large profit.

The Toronto Stock Exchange punished Newell's attempts to counter the short-selling raiders by suspending trading in Dynamic stock!

And Archie Newell, who had dared to rock the Bay Street boat, was punished. Dynamic would not be restored to trading, the T.S.E. pronounced, until and unless Newell resigned as president.

Newell of course resigned (though he remained a director of the company; the defeat was not total) and Frank Brown, another member of the controlling group, took over and made peace with the Bay Street establishment. Dynamic was listed again for trading.

Through the mid-sixties, Dynamic Petroleum was not a spectacular performer — just another speculative, resource-oriented operation and, as such, of very little interest to the Canadian financial community. The Company's shares traded up and down on both sides of the one dollar mark.

But the Dynamic group of companies acquired mineral rights on 1,500,000 acres in Athabasca and found indications that thorough exploration might turn up something of real value. Uranium, perhaps.

Dynamic, however, didn't have the money to find out. And Bay Street wasn't interested in financing mineral exploration in a remote corner of Saskatchewan.

So Dynamic turned to Gulf Oil, the U.S. giant, which had itself decided that it was an "energy" company, not just an oil company, and was therefore interested in uranium, an energy source with an enormous future potential.

In the words of a Gulf publicity handout, the Dynamic group, "Because they did not have the resources to continue the exploration of so vast an area, brought their findings to Gulf".

Gulf agreed to spend up to $750,000 over two years on explorations. Under the agreement, Dynamic had to be satisfied with 10% of profit until all costs were covered and 20% of profit thereafter.

Very quickly an enormous uranium ore body was discovered at Woolaston Lake in north-eastern Saskatchewan.

By 1970, Gulf was getting ready to bring the property into production. A $50 million mine and mill development was in the works. And a 49% interest in the property had been sold to Uranerz-Bonn, a German concern which simultaneously agreed to purchase four million pounds of uranium oxide a year from the property.

In August, 1970, Gulf nervously sought the approval of the Federal Government for its arrangements. Earlier in the year the Government had swiftly blocked Steve Roman's plans to sell his interest in the Dennison uranium property to foreigners, so Gulf was not unexpectedly anxious to get advance clearance before it went into the Canadian uranium business.

Gulf's worries were quickly set at rest. A spokesman from J.J. Greene's office said the company didn't need government approval. "Gulf Oil is exempt from Canada's regulations limiting foreign ownership of uranium properties because Gulf owned the property before the rules were announced in March."

Industry sources value the Woolaston Lake ore body at over one billion dollars.

Nobody in official Ottawa thought to comment that the property might have stayed in Canadian hands in the first place. If Dynamic Petroleum had been able to raise $750,000, they wouldn't have had to bring Gulf in. But they couldn't raise the money in Canada, so Gulf picked up the property for virtually nothing — and Canada quietly surrendered control of a significant portion of its resources of a mineral which the federal cabinet has decided is vital to our sovreignty.

On Bay Street there may have been a few regrets that Dynamic hadn't been able to finance its mineral explorations in Canada — but there was no evidence that anybody felt guilty.

The Banff and Dynamic stories are rather more typical than exceptional. The Canadian financial establishment has simply turned its back on Canada's natural resources potential. The economic elite's shortsighted lack of interest has been reflected in equally shortsighted taxation and other public policies.

And that's why Trade Minister Jean-Luc Pepin was obliged to reveal in the Commons not too many months ago that foreign interests now own 82.6% of our oil and gas production and 99.9% of our oil refining industry.

When James Miller Williams recovered the first gallon of kerosene from his primitive refinery in Oil Springs, Ontario, he couldn't have imagined that his fledgling venture was the forerunner of a multi-billion dollar industry. Nor, probably, would it ever have occurred to him that Canadians would be so foolish as to surrender complete control of this interesting and profitable new industry to foreigners.

But that, of course, is exactly what we did.

Electricity replaced kerosene as a source of light, but the internal combustion engine and, especially, the automobile created gigantic markets for petroleum products in the Twentieth Century.

For the first four and a half decades of the century, Canada meant very little to the worldwide petroleum industry. We were predominantly net importers of petroleum products, not producers.

But back in 1914, natural gas had been discovered in Alberta's Turner Valley. In 1936, Turner Valley began to produce oil. And after World War II, discoveries came thick and fast. Leduc in 1947. Redwater in 1948. And since then a stream of new discoveries as oil exploration moved east into Saskatchewan and north into northern Alberta and the Territories. Now, of course, since the rich "North Slope" discoveries in Alaska, the search for oil and gas has moved onto the Arctic coastline and the Arctic Islands.

In a belated effort to preserve for Canadians at least a portion of their inheritance of petroleum riches, the Government has established Panarctic Oils Ltd. Nineteen private companies hold 55% of the equity in Panarctic, but the government holds a dominant and controlling 45% interest. Panarctic now holds exploration rights on over 50 million acres in the Arctic islands, but already it has "farmed out" about three million acres to other – and most frequently foreign – firms. The theory, of course, is that Panarctic can make its own exploration money go farther by allowing other people to spend their money on exploring Panarctic's acreage. Perhaps. But it looks very much as though we're just repeating the same old mistake – assuming that Canada doesn't have enough capital to finance its own search for resources and letting the foreigners in to reap a rich harvest on their investment dollars.

Panarctic Oil will probably become one of the chosen investments of the long-awaited Canada Development Corporation. Since it appears that the CDC will be run as a business like any other by men who are members of the Canadian economic elite, the danger that we will surrender our last Arctic frontier to foreign control begins to loom large in the imagination.

On the basis of our financial community's despicable record, it would be, in fact, quite extraordinary if Canadians kept control of Arctic oil and gas resources.

Especially because the oil business is so thoroughly internationalized already. A handful of multi-national giants, mostly American but with Dutch and English representation, handle the free world's petroleum business in a special world in which profit is much more important than national boundaries or national interests. Canada is in the network.

As recently as 1955, Canadian refineries were processing more foreign than domestic crude oil. But in 1969, Canada's imports of crude oil were valued at $393 million, her domestic production at just over $1 billion, and her exports at $526 million (Canada exports oil from the West where production is heavy, imports it in the East — mostly from Venezuela — where production is negligible; it is cheaper to bring Venezuelan oil into Montreal by tanker than it would be to move Alberta oil to Montreal by pipeline).

In the context of traditional thinking about international trade and Canada's balance of payments, we're doing all right; we are net exporters of petroleum now and we earn more from our sales than we spend on our purchases. Because of the Americans' steadily growing appetite for oil and gas, there is no doubt that we will be able to find a market for as much as we can produce of either commodity.

But there are other factors to consider.

Of major importance, in the long run, is that the profits made from Canadian oil production and sales end up in foreign pockets.

More significant is the fact that Canadians simply don't own or control their multi-trillion dollar petroleum resources.

Even more important is the fact that foreign interests have gained control of enormously valuable assets at very little cost to themselves — and they have done so, to a remarkable degree, by using Canadian money for their purchases.

But looming over all else in long-term significance for the future of Canada is the image that our neighbours to the south have of themselves and of their own future. In the next chapter we look at what can only be called American imperialism.

THE NEW IMPERIALISM

A writer and historian in Yellowknife serves occasionally as a kind of official greeter and guide for groups of businessmen visiting the Northwest Territories on a Territorial Government industrial promotion junket.

Not too long ago he played host to a group from the American southwest.

What were they like?

"Very nice indeed. Fine people. Soft spoken, polite, interested in everything they saw, sympathetic to our problems, full of praise for our achievements in the Canadian North . . . but there *was* one peculiar thing. They spent a lot of time talking among themselves about what they were going to do with all the water they saw. And all the talk was about things like costs and engineering difficulties in moving the water south. They didn't even seem to realize that they were in a foreign country."

The American west and southwest are facing a water shortage. Canada has the world's largest supply of fresh water. What is more natural than for the Americans to think that all they have to do to use our water is solve the engineering problems?

After all, that's the way we've always done things together.

Canada's vast forests are cut down, processed in the pulp mills (35% of the industry was under U.S. control in 1963), and the newsprint is shipped south to feed the presses in the US.

77

Canada's minerals are mined and smelted (mining was 52% controlled by the Americans in 1963) and shipped south to keep the American factories running.

Oil and gas from our western fields (62% controlled by the Americans in 1963) are pumped through the pipelines to American markets as far east as Chicago.

And the Columbia River Treaty gave the American northwest vast new hydro power capacity from Canadian waters.

Lest anyone think that our position as a treasure-trove of resources for American industry is simply a matter of the natural and rational workings of a free enterprise economy on a continental basis, it is necessary to look at the *official* American attitude towards our resources.

The United States became great in the nineteenth century largely as a result of the exploitation of its own natural resources. The coal of west Virginia and the iron of the Mesabi Range built the American steel industry. Forests provided lumber. Western mountains yielded minerals. Texas, Oklahoma and California gushed with petroleum. The resources of the US half of the continent were plentiful and they enabled an energetic people to build the richest, most powerful nation the world has ever seen.

But then those resources began to run out.

A security-conscious US, embroiled in the Korean War and in what was seen as a world-wide battle against the threat of monolithic Communism, undertook a study of its natural resources. In June, 1952, the report of President Truman's Materials Policy Commission was released under the title, *Resources for Freedom.* Known as the Paley Report, the study recognized the fact that the US had, by the middle of the century, become a net importer of raw materials. Since the nation was not self-sufficient in "strategic" materials, it had to be assured of supplies of vital resources from abroad. James Laxer quotes this summation of the Paley Report*:

The Energy Poker Game by James Laxer. New Press, Toronto, 1970. The material presented in this chapter draws heavily on Mr. Laxer's excellent and disturbing book.

78

The over-all objective of a national Materials Policy for the United States should be to insure an adequate and dependable flow of materials at the lowest cost consistent with national security and with the welfare of friendly nations.

The reference to the "welfare of friendly nations" is a graceful public relations gesture, but it appears that the Americans are to decide what prices are consistent with the welfare of Canada and other "friendly nations".

The underdeveloped nations of the world — among which Canada must be included in the context of this discussion — are suppliers of raw materials to the developed nations. The developed nations process the commodities they have purchased and then export finished goods back to the underdeveloped nations.

But the two parties in this interchange are not possessed of equal bargaining power. In world trade, the prices of finished products have risen much more steeply over the past twenty-five years than have the prices of commodities and raw materials. The Ghanaians get proportionately less for the cocoa they sell to Britain than the British get for the pots and pans they sell to Ghana. Japan, Britain and Western Europe, the world's other industrialized trading economies, must be implicated in the growing price spread between raw materials and manufactured items, but the US, as the world's largest economic unit, is the trend-setter. The American economy is not closely controlled by the central government, and American foreign policy is largely formed through a chaotic and agonizing process of public debate. Nevertheless, it seems clear that the objectives of the Paley Report are being met. One way and another, the Americans have moved to obtain "an adequate and dependable flow of materials at the lowest cost".

Unfortunately, this policy places the future of the world in the most serious jeopardy. It is the rich nations which produce the manufactured products for the world, and the poor ones which supply the raw materials "at the lowest cost". The "have" nations grow richer, the "have-not" nations poorer. Locked in an apparently unbreakable cycle of poverty, the hundreds of millions of human beings who inhabit the so-called "developing" nations are now, thanks to the impact of global communications, embarking on a "revolution of rising expectations", they *know* that poverty is not necessarily the inescapable lot of mankind. The Chinese and the Cubans have largely opted out of the "free world's" economic system and are attempting, with greater or lesser success, to find their own way out of the poverty cycle. A marxist government in Chile has taken over that nation's copper mines. And the oil producers — the richest of the "poor" nations — have banded together to force the industrialized nations to pay higher prices for petroleum.

In this world-wide struggle, Canada occupies a unique position. We are the only "rich' nation with an economy dependent upon the sale of raw materials. Minerals alone account for more than a quarter of our total exports — with the US, Britain and the Common Market taking more than 80% of our total mineral exports, and Japan rapidly increasing its purchases.

We are affluent — the second or third richest people on the face of the earth in terms of per capita income. But we are — like Ghana, or Peru or the Philippines — dependent upon the industrialized nations for markets for our raw materials. And our prosperity is a thin and fragile thing, existing in the shadow of the US's voracious appetite for our raw materials and the Americans' determination to obtain those raw materials "at the lowest cost".

And the stakes are rising. On Space Ship Earth, resources, both renewable and non-renewable, are naturally limited. There is only so much oil under the salt domes, only so much fresh water in the world's rivers and lakes. As the world's population grows — and in particular as the United States' population and economy grows — the rush to control the world's resources, to keep them in friendly hands — is going to be a growing preoccupation for the Americans, both businessmen and government.

The American gross national product will reach one *trillion* dollars a year in 1971 or 1972. (American corporate profits, at over $80 billion a year, are about equal to Canada's total GNP.) And, the experts predict, the American GNP will reach *two* trillion dollars in about a decade and a half. In the long run, it will prove impossible for the Americans to maintain this rate of growth. But in the short run, before the bubble bursts, the American appetite for our resources will seem insatiable. And, unless we are more determined and more effective in our own defence than we have ever proved in the past, our political sovereignty will be eroded as thoroughly and as swiftly as our economic sovereignty has already been.

There are, of course, short-term advantages for us. When Mr. Greene and Mr. Chretien urge the Mackenzie route for a pipeline to take Alaska's petroleum to the "southern forty-eight", they see visions of northern development for Canada — new roads, new jobs, new townsites and, not least, an already paid-for pipeline system to bring Canadian oil to southern markets.

But just how much ultimate political control can Canadians expect to maintain over the three thousand miles of Mackenzie pipeline? The pipeline will be *owned* by companies under foreign control. And it will be seen — the debate is already conducted in these terms south of the border — as essential to American "national security". Could we, for example, replace Alaskan oil with Canadian Arctic oil in the Mackenzie pipeline? Could we, if we felt like it, close down the Mackenzie pipeline?

Not likely. James Laxer quotes an article that appeared in the US Army publication, *Military Review:*

If the mining potential of the Far North should be tapped, if harbour facilities and storage areas should be constructed, and if giant vessels regularly ply the North-west passage, then the northern region would suddenly become rich in military targets . . . the US defence posture — for the first time in history — would have to become northern oriented."

Fortunately, the *Manhattan's* voyage across the top of Canada was something less than a complete success, so the tankers are not yet plying our Arctic waters — and the American army's posture has not yet become "northern oriented".

But it certainly will be if the Mackenzie pipeline becomes a reality. Petroleum, in the thinking of American soldiers, politicians and economists, is a "strategic" resource; oil supplies must be secure if the American empire is to be secure.

It is necessary in this connection to think the unthinkable. If it comes to pass that Alaska's oil flows across Canada, and if we, in our wisdom, endanger that flow for whatever reasons we might have — then we will be confronted with an American response that will range from, at its mildest, the kind of economic retaliation that will simply destroy the fragile Canadian economy, to, at its most severe, armed invasion of Canada.

An armed invasion of Canada simply cannot be ruled out of consideration as a possible future development in Canada-US relations. The United States has a long and bloody tradition of resort to armed force to solve problems, real or apparent. Henry Steele Commager, the distinguished American historian, made this point recently in testimony before the US Senate Foreign Relations Committee in the context of the executive power of the US President:

Almost every instance of the use of presidential force in the past has been against small, backward, and distraught peoples: the situation today. Call the roll of the victims of presidential application of force in the past: Spanish Florida, Honduras, Santo Domingo, Nicaragua, Panama, Haiti, Guatemala, a China torn by civil war, a Mexico distraught by civil war, a Russia and a Vietnam riven by war. . . . Five times in the past ten years Presidents have mounted major military interventions in foreign nations without prior consultation with the Congress: the Bay of Pigs, the invasion of the Dominican Republic, the attacks on North Vietnam, Cambodia and Laos.

In his chillingly prophetic novel, *Killing Ground: The Canadian Civil War,** Ellis Portal tells the story of a bloody civil war that breaks out between Quebec and the rest of Canada after a determinedly separatist government wins power in Quebec City. The novel's conclusion is as disturbing as it is inevitable. The armed struggle within Canada results in the closing of the seaway. The Americans find their economic interests threatened by this development, so they ram a "peacekeeping resolution" through the United Nations and invade Canada. As the novel ends, French and English Canadians have joined together to make common cause against the invaders from the south.

Preposterous? Perhaps, but history has a way of surprising people. The "vital interests" of the British and French were threatened in the fifties when Egypt nationalized the Suez Canal (supertankers did not then exist to provide an economical alternative route around Africa for mideast oil). So Egypt was invaded. The steady and uninterrupted flow of oil from the north slope to an energy-hungry continental US is certainly going to be one of the "vital interests" of our neighbour to the south.

At this writing, Canadian politicians and diplomats face a genuine Hobson's choice. The Alaskan oil is going to come south whether we want it to or not. It's either going to come in an endless shuttle of supertankers through the hazardous and turbulent waters of Canada's west coast, with the near-certainty of accidental oil spills that will destroy the environmental balance of long stretches of our coast line, or it's going

*Peter Martin Associates, Toronto, 1968.

to come down the Mackenzie Valley in that $5 billion pipeline over which we will inevitably exercise substantially less than full sovereign control.

With very rare exceptions — Charles de Gaulle comes to mind — politicians simply do not think in terms of long-range effects. Perhaps the Mackenzie Valley pipeline to move Alaska's oil is in Canada's best interests. Perhaps in the long perspective of history it is our destiny to be enfolded in the warm and comfortable embrace of the American empire. Perhaps, in the world of *realpolitik*, we have no choice. But surely we must examine the alternatives, consider the implications, before we rush eagerly to our own dissolution.

Before World War II we were happy to sell electric power to the US on the basis of an annual contract. Came the War — for Canada before the US — and we needed every kilowatt we could lay our hands on as we feverishly tooled up for armaments production. The US refused to allow us to take back our power.

The Columbia River Treaty brought money to British Columbia. But it alienated, effectively forever, Canadian control over the upstream waters of the Columbia system — waters which were, and are, in Canadian territory.

As James Laxer says, "once you turn on the tap and begin supplying the Americans with water, you dare not ever turn it off. After all, even Fidel Castro stopped short of shutting off the water mains that supply fresh water to the American naval base at Guantanamo."*

*The Energy Poker Game. p. 42.

FRONT PAGE OF A NATION

"I have discovered," the newly-appointed editor said, "that we get most of our advertising from foreign-owned companies." He went on to wonder what effect his own well-known nationalist views were likely to have on the magazine's advertising revenues.

Most Canadian journalists and editors are men and women of the highest possible integrity. Few — if any — would keep a story out of their pages because an advertiser objected to it; in fact, they are more likely to react the other way to pressure of that sort — the threatening advertiser is likely to find the story he doesn't like given more prominence than it originally deserved.

But what kind of subtle pressures are at work? A newspaper or magazine that gets the reputation of being "cranky" in its editorial policies or its treatment of news is likely to lose advertising support. "Credibility" is one of the factors that goes into an advertiser's decision to buy — or not to buy — space in a particular journal. When the advertisers with the big dollars are people who consider that criticism of the foreign takeover of the Canadian economy is "cranky", then the editorial writers are affected. Subtly, not in any way they would want to talk about — or even think about — but affected they are.

What about the newspaper chains? Roy Thompson (Lord Thompson of Fleet) owns thirty Canadian daily newspapers.

The Southam chain includes papers in Ottawa, Hamilton, Winnipeg, Medicine Hat, Calgary, Edmonton, North Bay, and Vancouver. F.P. Publications owns the Winnipeg *Free Press,* the Calgary *Albertan,* the Lethbridge *Herald,* the Ottawa *Journal,* both the Victoria papers, the Vancouver *Sun,* and last but not least the Toronto *Globe and Mail.* In Canada, the proprietors of newspaper chains tend not to interfere directly in the editorial aspects of their investments. Newspapers are business and as long as the editors turn out a product that attracts readers and advertisers, the absentee owners don't much care about how the news is handled. But it is a common observation that papers belonging to chains tend to serve up a pretty bland diet.

In *The Uncertain Mirror,* Volume I of the Report of the Special Senate Committee on the Mass Media (the Davey Committee), the point is made that it isn't just the chain newspapers that subscribe to a "don't rock the boat" philosophy:

> No matter who owns the shares, a lousy newspaper is still a lousy newspaper. As Osgoode Hall Law Professor Desmond Morton recently observed: "It doesn't matter whether the North Bay *Nugget* belongs to Roy Thomson, Max Bell, or a local drygoods merchant. They are all, without a single exception, in the same kind of hands. They all belong to the Canadian business community and they all do what that community wants. And if Canadian businessmen assume an automatic, infallible identity between their views and those of every right-thinking Canadian, they are hardly unique among the oligarchs of history."

The only newspaper in Canada that has consistently warned of the consequences of foreign domination of the Canadian economy is the *Toronto Star.* The *Star,* perhaps not coincidentally, is also the largest newspaper in Canada, with a daily average circulation of more than 400,000 copies. It seems that the *Star's* vigorous defense of Canadian independence must meet with the approval of a great many readers in Central Canada. Many of the paper's advertisers undoubtedly disagree with the *Star's* editorial position on the issue, but they can't ignore the paper because of its enormous power as a sales and marketing medium.

It is ironical, though, that so few Canadian newspapers take a strong and consistent stand on the issue of foreign control of the economy, strange because the papers themselves are protected against the threat of foreign takeovers, foreign competition. Major American and British newspapers do reach our larger cities, but they do so in miniscule quantities. And the powerful British and American newspaper chains simply are not *allowed* to operate in the Canadian market.

The American, and to a lesser extent British, influence on what you read in your daily newspaper is more indirect, but it is nonetheless important.

Canadian papers — even the chains — either cannot spend or choose not to spend the money necessary to gather foreign news themselves. They maintain news bureaus in Washington and London and they will, on occasion, send senior reporters to cover major stories elsewhere. A few papers even keep permanent staffers in a few other countries (the *Globe and Mail* has had a man in Peking for more than a decade). But they rely for the bulk of their foreign news on foreign owned-and-operated news services. Associated Press, United Press International, and the Reuter Agency provide Canadian papers with most of their foreign coverage. (Canadian Press, a news agency jointly owned by the Canadian dailies, supplies a similar service for domestic and some foreign news).

The front page of the *Globe and Mail*, "Canada's National Newspaper", on March 17, 1971, had two stories from Associated Press (headed "Tricia to wed June 5 at the White House", and "Reward posted for POW rescue"), one from the *New York Times* and seven from the Reuter Agency. It would be

87

absurd to suggest that Canadian newspapers should stick to Canadian news; we're very much part of the world and we want and need to know what's going on elsewhere. *But more than half of the news stories in the newspaper were written by Americans, for Americans.* Canadian newspapers find it cheaper to use these stories as they come off the American wire than to cover the news themselves or even to rewrite from a Canadian perspective. We learn to see the world through American eyes.

Our magazines, by contrast, look at the world through Canadian eyes. *Maclean's, Saturday Night,* and *Chatelaine* are determinedly Canadian. They have to be; Canada is one subject not covered by the millions upon millions of U.S. periodicals that flood into Canada each year. The story of the destruction of our periodical press is one of the saddest in the whole history of the deterioration of the Canadian identity.

"Canada is probably the only large country in the world," Wilfred Eggleston of Carleton University wrote a decade ago, "whose inhabitants read more foreign magazines than domestic."

American periodicals have attracted Canadian readers for decades, but it was not until the 1950's that they began to attract Canadian advertising dollars as well. Advances in printing technology made it possible for magazines to produce "split runs", whereby the content — and particularly the advertising — in a magazine could be changed while the magazine was being printed. American advertisers were able to specify that they wanted their ad to be read in all copies going into particular states, but not in any of the copies going into other states. Soon the American magazine publishers realized that they could treat Canada as the subject of just one more split run. This made it possible for Canadian advertisers to buy space in popular American magazines, but have their ads appear only in copies coming to Canada. Immediately they did so, and the advertising revenue of

Canadian magazines fell precipitously.

In response to screams of pain, the Federal Government set up the O'Leary Commission to investigate the matter. Grattan O'Leary, a notably tough-minded journalist, recommended that advertisers be forbidden to deduct from their taxable income any money spent advertising in American "split runs". The Government adopted the recommendation. Businessmen were hit where it hurt — in the wallet — and the American "split-run" business quickly vanished.

With two exceptions. *Time* and *Readers' Digest* were exempted. Henry Luce, proprietor of the gigantic *Time-Life* empire, complained to Washington. Washington told Ottawa that if *Time* wasn't exempted from the new regulations the new Canadian-American auto pact wouldn't be accepted by the Americans. Ottawa weighed the alternatives. And Walter Gordon announced the exemption of *Time* and the *Digest* (Mr. Gordon is reliably reported to have said he found this announcement one of the most unpleasant duties he had ever undertaken).

Time and *Readers' Digest*, for their part, also made concessions. Both magazines established "editorial" offices in Montreal and undertook to do their Canadian printing in Canada. *Time* moved its coverage of Canadian news to the front of the magazine (and has even — as on the occasion of the Trudeau wedding — put a Canadian picture on its cover; these Canadian pictures, of course, do not appear on other editions of the magazine). *Readers' Digest* began to put "Canadian interest" boxes in the middle of their American stories and even made a stock offering in Canada so Canadians could participate in ownership (but not control) of the magazine and its associated book publishing and merchandising ventures.

The result was a disaster for Canadian magazines.

Time and *Readers' Digest* between them absorb 56% of all the money spent on consumer magazine advertising in Canada.

Mayfair and *Liberty* folded. *Canadian Homes,* once the most attractive "shelter book" in North America, became a slim newspaper supplement throwaway.

Maclean's consistently loses money. In 1969 the magazine stopped appearing fortnightly and became a monthly. At the same time, in a typically ironical Canadian development, *Maclean's* dropped its previous large format and went *"Time-size"* (yes, that's what they say in the industry: *"Time-*size"). This bit of cringing sycophancy helped for a while, but *Maclean's* is losing money again.

Saturday Night, the century-old Canadian journal of opinion, has been teetering on the edge of bankruptcy for years. It is kept alive by credit from Maclean-Hunter (if Maclean-Hunter put *Saturday Night* into bankruptcy, as they could readily do, they would probably face charges under the Combines Investigation Act; *Saturday Night* is the only Canadian competitor for *Maclean's*), by superhuman courage and desperate expedients on the part of its owners and managers, — and by frequent full-page advertisements by *Time!* (There seems to be no reciprocation: we never see a full-page ad in *Time* suggesting that *Saturday Night* might give Canadian readers a more appropriate view of Canadian public affairs; charity, after all, can only go so far.)

Only *Chatelaine,* and its teen-age spin-off *Miss Chatelaine,* among the tiny handful of Canadian consumer magazines, manage to earn a profit sufficient to keep them out of trouble. Aimed primarily at women (though it has an astonishingly high male readership), *Chatelaine* is not competing head-on with *Time* for the same advertising. And, as the only Canadian magazine in its field, it isn't competing head-on with anyone, so it rakes in the advertising dollars. A quick and incomplete survey of the March, 1971, issue of *Chatelaine* indicates that the magazine gets six times as much advertising from foreign-owned companies as from Canadian (the survey is incomplete because it was impossible to determine the nationality of the advertisers buying approximately thirteen pages of advertising). Foreign firms or their subsidiaries provided about twenty-nine pages of the magazine's advertising; Canadian-owned firms (including the CBC and "Your Hydro") bought five and one-half pages. Kraft Foods alone, with five pages, almost matched the *total* Canadian-owned advertising content.

There are indications that the Federal Government wants to revoke the exemption *Time* and *Readers' Digest* enjoy under the advertising regulations. Now that the Americans are so involved in the auto pact that they cannot back out (and the terrifying Henry Luce has gone to meet his Maker), this might prove to be politically possible. But the Canadian consumer magazine industry has been so ravaged in the past twenty years that it is unlikely ever to flourish again. About all that we can hope for is the survival and growth of the three consumer magazines we have left.

One of the blows suffered by magazines was, of course, administered to them by television. Magazines have had a tough time of it in recent years in every country in which television advertising is allowed. The Canadian story, therefore, is not unique, just uniquely bad.

For forty years and more, Canadians have worried that the Americans would come to control the enormously persuasive electronic media. Give them control of our airwaves and it would be game over. So it was in the 1930's when the Radio League of Canada fought hard and long for the establishment of a national, publicly-owned broadcasting network in Canada. And so it still was at the end of the sixties when the new and formidable Canadian Radio and Television Commission produced a series of rulings that stripped foreign-controlled firms of all their rights to own radio, television or cable companies in Canada. There have always been powerful forces on the other side, but this is one battle which has been fought and won in the national interest.

Still, the subtle insinuation of alien values into Canadian life continues. Both our television networks carry a heavy load of American-originated programming. Our cable companies have flourished because they were able to put sharp, clear pictures from American stations into Canadian homes (there are U.S. stations in Vermont, Buffalo, Minnessota and the State of Washington that almost certainly wouldn't exist if they had to depend on local audiences on their own side of the border; they live on Canadian viewers, Canadian advertisers).

The CRTC has moved in this area too. Comparatively tough Canadian content rules have been imposed on both television and radio broadcasting. Some of the ground previously lost in broadcasting has been recovered. It is, however, distressing that so few Canadians seem pleased; broadcasters believe that Canadians want to watch American situation comedies, listen to American bubblegum rock music. This may be because we present few alternatives; in most fields, Canadian producers and artists simply imitate American models, with inferior results (to their credit, Canadian performers have broken new ground in serious rock music and have received international recognition; this may be because this field is open to new talent and is not the exclusive preserve of exploitation by gigantic corporations).

If television gets too much for you, there is always the neighborhood picture palace. In Canada, there are nine companies significantly involved in film distribution. Seven of these are foreign-owned. Feature films cannot be successfully financed, produced and shown unless distribution can be arranged. Nobody is going to pay to see your picture unless the picture is booked into a theatre. It isn't booked into a theatre unless a distributor arranges to handle it for you. And the distributors simply aren't interested in Canadian films.

This, too, may be changing as a result of government action. On the initiative of two Secretaries of State, one Liberal the other Conservative, the Government of Canada finally created the Canadian Film Development Corporation. This body, provided with public money, was authorized to put dollars into Canadian feature film production. Film-makers no longer had to rely exclusively on the approval of distributors to finance their films; they could get money from the CFDC. French Canada immediately blossomed forth with a torrent of feature films, some of them very good. In English-speaking Canada, the films were fewer and worse, but a beginning was made.

The most successful firm to benefit from the creation of the CFDC was Montreal-based Cinepix which, through a variety of production packaging deals, proved that Canadians could make "skin flicks" as well as anybody else. Cinepix's "sexploitation" products were something totally new in Canadian feature film production — they made money.

Late in 1970, control of Cinepix was sold to a New York firm.

The sale of Cinepix went almost unnoticed by the public, but the sale of two other Canadian "cultural" corporations produced a notable degree of public concern.

For many years, the W.J. Gage book publishing firm had relied heavily on books developed and written in the U.S. for the products it sold to Canadian school systems. The famous *Dick and Jane* primers, originating with the Scott, Foresman Company in the U.S., taught millions of Canadian children their early reading skills. In September, 1970, the Scott, Foresman people told W.J. Gage that they were going to be taken over. If Gage didn't sell its textbook business to Scott, Foresman, then the latter would simply set up its own operation in Canada and leave Gage without books to sell.

Gage sold — and Gage director Allistair Gillespie, a Liberal

MP, resigned from the board in protest.

Meanwhile, the Ryerson Press, Canada's oldest book publishing house, was up for sale. Conceived by Egerton Ryerson and operated for decades as the Methodist Book Room, the Ryerson Press had been an important Canadian educational and cultural institution for more than a century. But its proprietors, the Board of Stewards of the United Church, were unwilling — or unable — to supply the capital that the Press needed if it was to compete successfully with the Canadian branch plants of the giant American school book publishers. Ryerson executives, when it became clear that the Church wanted out, canvassed desperately for a Canadian buyer. None could be found. And the Ryerson Press was sold to McGraw-Hill Canada Limited, a wholly-owned subsidiary of McGraw-Hill, Incorporated.

The Ryerson sale prompted the creation of a loose association of the remaining Canadian-owned book publishing houses, three middle-sized, established firms and a double handful of small, new (and generally nationalist) houses. The public agitation of the Canadian-owned book publishers led to a two-day conference in Ottawa called by the Secretary of State and to the creation of a Royal Commission in Ontario, both concerned with the future of book publishing in Canada.

Significantly, the established trade association of the book publishers, the Canadian Book Publishers Council, remained absolutely silent on the whole issue of the foreign takeover of our book publishing firms. A majority of the member firms in the CBPC are either the wholly-owned branch plants of foreign publishers or are agent-importers dependent upon the sale in Canada of books published abroad.

Book publishing, as an economic activity, contributes very little to our gross national product — less than one-tenth of one percent of the g.n.p. But it is disproportionately important to the maintenance of a national sense of identity. Books — and newer, related teaching materials — provide our children with their basic knowledge of their nation, its history, its geography, its peoples and its way of life. The Canadian-owned publishing houses argue that the instruction of our children is too important an activity, too central to the Canadian experience, to be left in the hands of foreigners. They point to shocking instances of the increasing American influence in our schools — Canadian children reading about what fun it is to learn to shoot guns with the marines, Canadian children learning about Canada's national sport in books published south of the border where the game is called "ice-hockey", Canadian children learning their own country's history from textbooks which are superficial adaptations of American history books.

In the field of adult reading — the kind of books, like this one, that people buy in bookstores or borrow from libraries — the Canadian publishers insist that the great issues of Canadian life will only be argued out between covers if there are Canadian-owned publishing houses to bring out the books.

Although it can be argued that the book publishers' value to the nation is more cultural than economic, nevertheless the problems the few remaining Canadian publishers face are remarkably similar to the problems Canadian enterprises face in every kind of business from petroleum exploration to funeral parlours.

The Canadian publishers simply cannot find or raise in Canada the capital they need to compete with the American giants. Canadian financial institutions — controlled by the "economic elite" — compete eagerly to provide Canadian funds for the branch-plant subsidiaries of American corporations, but the cash-box closes with a snap when a Canadian entrepreneur needs capital.

The Canadian manager of a new branch plant book publishing operation, the Canadian subsidiary of Van Nostrand Rinehold which is, in turn, a subsidiary of the gigantic American conglomerate, Litton Industries, reveals that he has no need to import capital from his parent corporation in the U.S. — the Canadian banks provide him with all he needs. At the same time Jack McClelland, president of McClelland & Stewart, the largest and most dynamic of the remaining Canadian owned book publishers, announced at a press conference that his firm was for sale; McClelland and Stewart was unable to find the capital it needed to continue to operate. (Another of those Canadian ironies: Jack McClelland is one of the founders of the Committee for an Independent Canada but he was forced by economic circumstances to consider the possibility that he might have to sell his firm to the Americans). On the urgent recommendation of the Ontario Royal Commission on Book Publishing, an enquiry established in the aftermath of the Ryerson sale, the Ontario government provided almost a million dollars to McClelland and Stewart, thereby enabling the firm to stay in Canadian hands.

The Ontario government's timely decision to make funds available to McClelland and Stewart indicates a commitment made on behalf of the people-as-a-whole, and a judgment that book publishing is of such importance to the survival of the Canadian nation that it could not be left exclusively in the hands of foreigners. Government, of course, moved in reluctantly, and only because the required backing simply was not available from sources in the private sector.

The experience of another Canadian cultural asset should be mentioned in this context. The Royal Ontario Museum is a world-respected institution. Situated in midtown Toronto, the ROM found its financial resources dwindling alarmingly in relation to the demands made on it by the growing and increasingly learning-oriented Metropolitan community. So the ROM's imaginative, aggressive Director, Dr. Peter Swann, penned a letter to three hundred large American corporations with well-established Canadian subsidiaries. Swann's plea was that these corporations were making money out of Canada and should, therefore, feel some kind of responsibility for the quality of Canadian life, a feeling of responsibility that could be acted upon, in this context, by making a contribution to the Royal Ontario Museum. To his three hundred letters, Swann got two replies – and no money.

If you live and work in Akron or Pittsburgh, Canada is a place where money can be made, not a cultural entity for which you feel any responsibility. Charity, as the old saying goes, begins at home. And home for a shockingly large percentage of Canadian industry, isn't Canada.

Newspapers filling their pages with stories written by Americans and for Americans. A magazine industry virtually destroyed by unimpeded foreign competition. A film industry which, in spite of government funding, is dependent upon distribution facilities almost totally controlled beyond Canada's borders. Radio, television and cablecasting systems which depend heavily upon foreign programming packages and the advertising dollars of foreign-owned corporations. And a book publishing industry which is in immediate danger of extinction. These are the media of communication which transmit ideas, entertainment and creative expression from one mind to another. They are also the media that perform the vital function of carrying the Canadian story from one generation to the next. As they fall more and more under American domination the chances of Canada's survival as anything more than a quaint geographical expression become slimmer and slimmer.

SINS OF OMISSION,

SINS OF COMMISSION

Early in 1971, A.K. Velan of Velan Engineering Limited of Montreal wrote to the Toronto Star:

Our company is not up for sale, but if policies emanating from Ottawa persist, the possibility of our becoming a US-owned firm exists.

We are the largest valve manufacturer in Canada. Sales this year were $16 million; potential sales four years from now are $40 million. There are 500 people currently employed, and a potential exists for 1,500.

Our plant is ultra-modern, highly automated and we have an extensive research department. More than 80 percent of our goods are exported, mainly to the United States. We produce a complete line of high-pressure valves for fossil and nuclear power stations, shipbuilding, oil, and petrochemical and chemical industries, etc. Our present ownership is 100 per cent Canadian.

What would be the reasons behind the decision of a proud Canadian to put his company up for sale, probably to a US buyer? Mainly disenchantment with some government policies.

First, there is a lack of policy on Canadian ownership.

Secondly, I would like to cite the sudden and unexpected decision to re-evaluate the Canadian dollar last May (1970). Jean-Luc Pépin, federal minister of trade and industry, declared in Parliament shortly after the announcement was made that any Canadian export industry affected would obtain help. When our application was made (we suffered a loss of $800,000 on a backlog of $12 million US orders), we were told that Mr. Pépin's criteria for assistance would be danger of bankruptcy or a substantial lay-off of employees (minimum 25 per cent).

Our opinion that dangerous deterioration of cash flow should also receive consideration was rejected. We have in the past been able to expand and create jobs from re-investing profits efficiently. This desirable situation has now been seriously affected.

Third, there is no policy of support for exporting, secondary industries — the backbone of the Canadian economy. (Some countries, such as Germany and Italy, provide 3 per cent to 7 per cent export subsidies. In Canada, we hit exporters with the re-evaluation of currency as well as support damaging imports, thus creating unemployment.)

Fourth, there is a lack of a generally acceptable Buy Canadian policy.

Fifth, the government rejected our application for reduced duty on large, sophisticated forgings for nuclear valves, which can be obtained only from one source in the US and are re-exported to the US.

Sixth, Canada lacks a proper fiscal policy for succession duties. There is actually a diminishing incentive for second generations to continue successful family businesses.

Seventh, some of the proposals in the White Paper on Tax Reform would hurt secondary industries.

Eighth, there is the surtax on corporations and personal income tax.

Ninth, Canada lacks an efficient regional development programme. To illustrate what I mean, I would like to cite the offer received from Regional Development Minister Marchand of $750,000 on our project of a $3,500,000 plant in Granby, Quebec with 80 percent payable when production commences. Actually, we could go to Ohio and receive complete financing of the project based on a 25-year mortgage. Gifts are not required, but full financing is a must.

Tenth, there is no policy on unemployment.

Eleventh, there is a lack of protection for employers against unreasonable strikes and abuse by labour unions. Socialist Sweden recently accepted an anti-strike legislation. Why not Canada?

I could actually go for much longer, but what I really want to do is to appeal to the Prime Minister to use his ability and sophistication to make this greatest country of all, Canada, even better for us and future generations.

What kind of comment can possibly be made on a statement like that?

Perhaps the best one is provided by Irving Goodman, president of Aimco Industries, a large and profitable manufacturer of automobile brake shoes.

Mr. Goodman said he needed money to expand and couldn't find it in Canada. His company looked like a good bet for investors — it made just over $1 million on sales of $21 million in 1970 — but Canadian sources of further financing were unhelpful. "We went to the Department of Trade and Commerce's, General Assistance Board," reports Mr. Goodman, "and all they gave us was the run-around. Finally they told us that because we're not starving we should raise money on the public market." Rejected by the government, Goodman went to Bay Street, to talk to the underwriters. "They weren't even willing to evaluate our assets for collateral," he reports. "None of them wanted to look at a so-called junior industrial unless it was available at bargain prices."

Goodman says that, even after he was rejected by both public and private sources in Canada, he didn't run to the US hat in hand to look for the money he needed to keep his business growing. "They came to us," he says.

Control of Aimco was sold, on March 31, 1971, to IT&T,

the gigantic US conglomerate, International Telephone and Telegraph.

Mr. Velans powerfully-expressed indictment of the package of Canadian government policies which militate against Canadian control of Canadian industry is vividly underscored by the depressing list of takeovers. Behind every terse announcement of a takeover there is a human story — a story of businessmen, responsive to a complex network of obligations, commitments and personal relations, attempting to solve a problem, and finding that Canadian law and Canadian government policies load the dice in favour of a solution that rewards a sale to the foreigners.

Recently, a young Toronto lawyer revealed the fact to friends, that he had suddenly became a millionaire.

The young lawyer's family came from central Europe in the 1880's and settled in Toronto, believing in the promise of the New World and eager to work to realize that promise for themselves.

His grandfather, patriarch of the clan, died in the great flu epidemic immediately after the First World War, leaving behind sons who had nothing going for them except their talent and their energy and an inherited belief in Canada's potential. The sons were young and inexperienced, but they were eager to work. The young lawyer's uncle was, on his father's death, the oldest of the clan, so he took over control of the small clothing manufacturing business the grandfather had developed. Within a few years the original firm was bankrupt; in the fiercely competitive "rag trade" inexperienced young men do not succeed easily.

But this family was not the kind to give up easily. Two of the brothers and a third partner established a new firm in the mid-twenties. The young lawyer's father, the baby of the family, joined the struggling firm some years later by buying out the unrelated partner.

The firm survived the depression, the war and the postwar

boom. One brother dropped out and was replaced by another, compatible, outside partner.

The owner-managers had committed their lives to the business. They manufactured and sold a broad line of workaday clothing items under their own name, and also produced a higher-priced line under a franchised American brand name. Their business grew and prospered. From something like the proverbial pushcart start, they had grown remarkably by the late sixties.

A loan from the Industrial Development Bank enabled them to move manufacturing operations from cramped and inadequate facilities in downtown Toronto to an efficient new plant outside Toronto's core. The company's careful mix of quality, value and service (plus, let it be added, aggressive marketing) had given them a large share of the Canadian market. The new Toronto plant was supplemented by two other factories in Québec and one more in Ontario.

In 1968 the company operated four plants, employed more than fifteen hundred Canadians, supplied good clothing to Canadians at reasonable prices and had gross sales in the neighborhood of twenty million dollars.

Two years later the firm was sold to Americans.

Why?

The answer is to be found not in any internal characteristics of the company, nor in the immediate wishes and desires of its owner-managers.

It is to be found in the structure of the Canadian financial community and in the minutiae of Canadian tax legislation.

The partners had, over forty years, taken almost nothing out of their enterprise. They had worked hard and their company had generated respectable earnings. But the earnings were regularly reinvested in further growth. By deferring consumption, the partners had produced some very specific economic results. The profit margin in the mass-market clothing business is not large; it runs at about two percent.

Two percent profit on $20 million in sales might have allowed the partners to join the jet set, at least in a minor way, if they had chosen to take the money out. But they didn't. They weren't taking out four hundred thousand a year; they were taking an amount much closer to one-tenth of total profit, and leaving the rest in the company to finance further growth, more jobs and, ultimately, more taxes.

By foregoing most of the profit, by plowing it back into the business, the partners had created a large, efficient Canadian enterprise, manufacturing in two provinces and selling in ten — and around the world.

But the partners knew what Ben Franklin had said in 1789.

"Nothing," Franklin said, "can be said to be certain except death and taxes."

Death comes to all men, and men who wish their works to survive them must make allowances for mortality. Taxes, however, are another matter. A human invention, they reflect human understandings, human objectives.

Love — to use a disturbing word in an economic discussion — also entered into the equation.

The partners who had created the firm in the twenties and who had built it through the four decades that followed were forced to solve an equation in which the only known quantities were death, taxes and love.

They would have preferred to pass on the firm, intact, to the next generation.

But Canadian estate taxes prevented that. The partners, because they had taken very little out of the company, had severely limited outside resources. When death claimed them, they realized, government would be demanding succession duties and estate taxes — and would be demanding settlement in cash. But neither the partners nor the company had surplus cash. Money had always been an instrument of growth, not a commodity to be hoarded.

Unless drastic steps were taken, therefore, death would

have produced a distress sale of the firm to satisfy government demands. At best a change of ownership (with the buyer in the catbird seat when it came to negotiating price), and at worst the breakup and disappearance of the firm.

So they could not pass on the firm intact to their heirs.

Nor, they concluded, could they hold onto it and plan, over a period of years, to look for a buyer whose interests and talents and capacities were compatible with their own. The uncertainties presented by the Carter Report, by Mr. Benson's White Paper on taxation, by the nightmarish obscurity of governments' threatened but unspecific future demands upon private capital gains, all these uncertainties made a leisurely consideration of the alternatives impossible for the partners.

In their own judgment — at the end of the sixties — they had to sell fast before the ground rules changed beneath them in unpredictable ways.

So the company was put up for sale. The partners wanted an offer which would let them do what they did well — run a successful clothing manufacturing business — and which would also provide economic security for their children and families. Why, after all, had they struggled and taken risks for so many years except for their families?

When the news got about that the company was for sale, six serious bidders appeared on the doorstep, two of them Canadian, the other four American. The Canadians, from innate caution and because they couldn't, at the time, deduct their acquisition costs from taxable income, offered prices significantly below the Americans.

In fact, the eventual American purchasers were able to offer *twice as much money* as the Canadian bidders could muster.

The deal was a good one for the partners. They kept title to the company's real estate and generated a good, secure income by leasing the property and facilities back to the

American buyers. They acquired convertible debentures issued by the new owners and were able, therefore, to realize their capital gain over a period of time (without fear of a capital gains tax, because the deal was consumated before such a tax was imposed in Canada) and to pass on the proceeds to their children. And, perhaps most importantly in terms of human motivation and satisfaction, they were retained on five-year management contracts, contracts which enabled them to continue doing what they knew best how to do — manufacturing and selling clothing.

For the children and families too, the arrangement was a good one. My friend was embarrassed by his sudden status as a millionaire, but his financial future is secure. The money flowing through to him from the convertible debentures generated by the sale of the family firm is being placed in real estate, to earn about 10 percent a year, a nice hedge against inflation.

But this young, socially-conscious lawyer feels less uncomfortable about his own economic security than he does about the effects of the foreign takeover of his family's firm. Using their first Canadian acquisition as a base, the Americans have taken over, in the first eighteen months since the deal was signed, no fewer than six other Canadian-owned firms. What is more, the American parent now has a foothold in Commonwealth markets through ownership of Canadian corporations; exports are growing precipitously, a development which the conventional Canadian economic wisdom welcomes but which, in this instance, ultimately puts more Canadian money in American pockets.

Who can we blame? A man's first responsibility in every society is to his own loved ones. The family we have described above might have refused to sell out, but in so doing they would have been depriving themselves — and, more importantly to them, their children — of the maximum return from the fruits of their labours. They sold to the Americans not by deliberate choice but because Canadian tax legislation is so contrived that selling out to foreign interests has been a more attractive solution to the succession problem than keeping the concern in Canadian hands.

How can this be? Why would the nation's legislators build up a complex of rules, regulations and laws that militate against the retention of Canadian enterprises in Canadian hands, that positively encourage the transfer of ownership of successful corporations to foreign interests? No credible answer is available, because the situation itself abuses credibility.

But it is at least suggestive that the men who owned and managed the company described above had one further problem. Capital for expansion was not available to them on reasonable terms from Canadian sources. Now that they have sold out, they find that the company has no trouble securing expansion and acquisition capital. In Canada, when Canadians owned the firm, the doors of the Canadian money managers were closed. But when the Americans took over, the hundred-percent-Canadian red carpet was rolled out for them at the temples of finance.

Is there a vicious international conspiracy? Are Canada and the Canadian economy being willfully destroyed by a tight network of foreign imperialists and Canadian quislings, both economic and political? Of course not.

But the effects are such that a paranoid interpretation of this sort begins to seem seductively plausible.

Now that the clothing manufacturer we have described above is in American hands, we can look forward to the implementation of management programs aimed at efficiency and rationalization.

If there is a downturn in the clothing business, which plant do you suppose will be closed — the plant in North Carolina or the plant in Valleyfield?

Valleyfield, of course . . . .

It's little wonder that the young millionaire lawyer is embarrassed and uncomfortable.

In cases like the one just described, the tax-and-law environment in which a closely-held Canadian manufacturing company operates almost looks as though it were deliberately constructed to force transfer of ownership into foreign hands. But, in truth, this hostile environment was created over many years in which a casual and almost accidental collection of government measures were implemented — often with little or no thought for their less obvious implications. Succession duties and estate taxes, for example, have been seen by Canadian governments as tools for preventing the accumulation of a socially-undesirable amount of wealth in a few hands (and also, of course, as a handy method for adding to government revenue). The fact that our estate taxes have worked to alienate ownership of our industries was an accidental — and largely unanticipated — by-product of muddle-headed legislative thinking.

But the involvement of successive Canadian governments in creating the climate in which natural resource corporations operate looks much more like the implementation of a deliberately-conceived programme — and a programme which has been, in its workings, an irresponsible betrayal of the best interests of Canada and Canadians.

Eric Kierans resigned from the Trudeau government for a number of reasons, but in his public statements he made it clear that his overriding concern was the government's mismanagement of the Canadian economy.

Kierans describes a situation which makes Canadians look like fools.

In our rush to see Canada's non-renewable resources exploited (so we can continue to be the world's richest underdeveloped nation), we have fallen all over ourselves in our eagerness to welcome the foreigners in. We have handed over a dominant position in both mining and petroleum to non-Canadian owners. This might conceivably have been good for Canada, as well as for the foreign owners, if we had derived any large-scale and permanent benefits from the rapid exploitation of our resources. But we haven't had the wit to do even that.

The resource industries are heavily capital-intensive, but they create comparatively few jobs. Hard-rock mining still employs a reasonable number of workers in relation to capital committed (and, it must be remembered, creates an additional six or seven above-ground jobs for every man in the mines), but neither the Saskatchewan potash industry, nor the big new coal mines in the Rockies, nor certainly the oil and gas wells of the Prairies employ a significant number of workers in relation either to the amount of capital invested or the value of the commodities extracted.

Eric Kierans argues that the welcome mat we have put out for foreign resource-exploiters distorts the structure of our economy and condemns us to a tragically high and permanent level of unemployment.

But that is only part of the story. We have not had enough new jobs from foreign-controlled resource development, nor have we had enough revenue. In both petroleum and mining, truly extraordinary tax benefits are offered. Depreciation and depletion allowances for the extractive industries result in their paying, according to a *Toronto Star* survey, between nine and twelve percent of their profits in taxes while manufacturing concerns pay between forty and fifty percent of their profits to the government.

There is, of course, a sound reason why the extractive industries should receive tax concessions. A mine or an oil field can have a profitable life of as little as twenty years, or even less, and then there's nothing left, whereas a foundary or a textile mill can, in theory at least, go on forever, just renewing equipment and buildings as required.

But one of the side effects of this impeccable economic logic is that low tax rates in the extractive industries enable the large, foreign corporations to accumulate capital very rapidly and thereby to increase their control of Canada's natural resources through further exploration or outright acquisition.

And, inevitably, the money that the government doesn't take from the natural resource industries is, instead, taken from other pockets — yours and mine and the corporations in other fields of endeavour. The spread of tax rates also means that we sell our nickel and our natural gas cheaply beyond our borders but we pay high prices for the products of our own highly-taxed manufacturing industries.

We seem to delight in collecting the least revenue from the industries which are most dominated by foreigners and which provide the fewest jobs for Canadians. If a Canadian politician ran on a platform advocating a policy of this kind he would be laughed off the hustings. But successive federal and provincial governments have structured our laws to do just this.

The true absurdity, of course, is that none of this is necessary. Canada has bountiful natural resources in an increasingly resource-starved world. Demand fluctuates dramatically from year to year, but over the long haul we would have no trouble selling our iron and coal and petroleum at our asking prices. The men who run the multinational corporations in the extractive industries are, by and large, decent people who want to buy and sell and build and make a reasonable profit in the process and they are willing to play the business game under any reasonable set of rules. Down there in Dallas, they must think we are either incompetent or crazy. The Canadian government bargains with less wit and less determination than the most backward, illiterate Persian Gulf sheik.

Joseph de Maistre said that, "Every nation has the government that it deserves." But do the Canadian people really get the government they deserve? Do we really deserve a succession of governments that, regardless of party, seem hell bent on making it as difficult as possible for Canadians to retain control of their own economy?

International economics is a complex, subtle subject beyond, perhaps, the present capabilities of human beings to comprehend completely. From Breton Woods to the Gnomes of Zurich, some of the best minds in the world have been devoted to the task of keeping international trade and international monetary relations working as well as possible. But the task is an exceedingly difficult one. Each nation has its own resources, its own skills, its own life-style, its own social and economic objectives, and reconciling these is far from easy. Dislocations occur.

In the spring of 1971, an accumulation of factors produced a crisis in the American dollar. On the surface — and most of the news stories failed to go below the surface — the international monetary crisis appeared to be upward pressure first on the German Mark and then on the Japanese Yen. The Europeans met and deliberated and looked for solutions. The Japanese defended their currency resolutely.

But behind the headlines lay the truth. Around the world the Americans were spending beyond their resources. Their tragic commitment to war in Southeast Asia was taking its toll. The young soldiers shipped home in pine boxes draped in Old Glory were the most visible sign of the nation's agony. But the steady weakening of what had been the world's strongest currency was a hidden cost of the wars. The U.S. was spending more abroad than it was earning, and at home it appeared impossible to control relentless inflation. The U.S. refused to devalue the dollar in relation to the world's other trading currencies. And when the Americans refused to devalue (a tough and embarrassing process that the British, French, Germans, Italians, even the Canadians have gone through in the past), only one other solution was possible — other currencies had to be increased in value in relation to the American dollar. And that is what happened.

For Canada, an aggravation. The Canadian dollar is strong — perhaps too strong in relation to the American dollar — but we are so much a part of the American sphere of economic influence that we have suffered with the U.S.

Because we have tied ourselves so closely to the U.S. economy, we are inextricably involved in their problems. The Canadian financial community, the economic elite, the Canadian government, have allowed us — encouraged us — to become an economic dependency of the U.S. As the U.S. goes, so goes Canada.

Of course, total economic independence is impossible for any country. The world's economy is too sophisticated and too integrated for any nation to escape the effects of changes in the economic health of any other nation. But Canada's position is unique by virtue of our dependence upon a single trading partner, and a partner, moreover, which has acquired control of large and important sections of our domestic economy.

The wooing of foreign capital continues unabated. In spite of the overwhelming evidence that we are now generating enough net savings to meet our development capital requirements . . . in spite of the obvious dangers inherent in our becoming even more closely tied to the precarious American economy and the troubled American society . . . in spite of the distortions produced in the Canadian economy as it is operated to meet the objectives of corporations domiciled abroad . . . and in spite of the fact that foreign ownership means that the profits of our enterprise flow away from us in torrents . . . in spite of all these factors, thoroughly responsible Canadians still eagerly put out the welcome mat for foreign investors and developers.

Harry Flemming, executive vice-president of the Atlantic Provinces Economic Council, attacked Canadian economic nationalists in a speech to the Greater Moncton Chamber of Commerce. He contended that the nationalists are strongest in Ontario and that "we must not assume that the interests of the Atlantic provinces are necessarily those of Ontario". "Economic nationalists," he said, "have a habit of skimming lightly over the issue of regional development. They quickly utter the magic words, Canadian Development Corporation, and then move into the higher realms of theory and emotion."

Premier Robert Bourassa of Quebec vigorously defended his province's continuing search for foreign capital shortly after he introduced his $6 billion James Bay power plan. He told reporters that his province needed foreign capital to reach full employment and higher living standards and to bridge the gap between the rich and the poor. And, he argued, even if foreign capital were not necessary for Quebec, it would be wrong for the province to go without the skills and knowledge that foreign capital brings with it.

And, from further west, here is part of a television discussion between Premier Harry Strom of Alberta and questioners Bruce Wilkinson (an economist at the University of Alberta), Charles Lynch of Southam News Services, and Ron Collister of the CBC:

> *Lynch:* You don't feel your sovereignty is invaded by the high degree of American — well, I was going to use the word ownership — of American entrepreneurship in Alberta.
>
> *Strom:* No, I don't think so, and of course let me make it very clear because I think that this could lead to a misunderstanding as to my views on whether or not I'm interested in Canadian investment. And I want to make it very clear that, as far as I'm concerned, we welcome Canadian investment (emphasis added) and of course . . . .
>
> *Lynch:* Well, it would be phenomenal if you said you didn't. That's a non-statement.
>
> *Strom:* I made it for the reason that I am defending the inflow of investment to our province and I don't want it misunderstood as being *against* something. And

of course it should go without saying, but I want it to be on the record.

Lynch: Well you're not upset about U.S. investment. Do you feel that the rest of the country, and the Federal Government indeed, is spending an undue amount of time worrying about this very thing, about the American penetration of our economy?

Strom: I think that they are. I think that they are to the extent that they could in fact slow down development to a great extent by planning the picture in such a way that investors will feel that there is no future for investment and development in this Province.

Why is it that, in spite of all the clear dangers and the obviously high costs of importing American capital and surrendering control of our industries and our natural resources, responsible Canadians in the Maritimes, Quebec and the West are going out of their way to make public statements, emphasizing their eagerness to accept American capital?

The answer is complex in detail, but in outline it is very simple.

From the mid-thirties, when the Toronto Stock Exchange absorbed the old Standard Exchange, the Toronto-based financial community — peopled by the members of John Porter's "economic elite" as described in an earlier chapter — with its fellow-travellers ensconced in Montreal and a few other major cities, has increasingly dominated the pattern and direction of Canadian investment. Continentalism has appealed to members of the economic elite. They like the money the Americans pay, fast and in large quantities, so they have induced Canadians to invest their savings south of the border while, simultaneously, helping foreigners to acquire Canadian properties.

Essential to this profitable programme has been the destruction of competitive sources of speculative financing in Canada. The Winnipeg Exchange was wiped out. Calgary — the natural locus for the marshalling of risk capital for oil and gas exploration — has been reduced to near impotence. The Maritimes, where one might think the logic of a local stock exchange was irresistible, found its brokerage houses bought out by the big, rich Toronto-Montreal firms which, of course, were not even remotely interested in supporting a small, local exchange.

The resulting distortions of investment patterns are so bizzare that we wouldn't believe them possible — if we weren't so used to them!

Politicians and businessmen in all the provinces east and west of Ontario, despairing of finding in Canada the capital they need for development, turn to U.S. and overseas sources for funds — but at the same time the savings of their own citizens are funneled into Toronto and promptly sent out of the country. On a per capita basis Canadians have invested $561 each in the United States, while Americans have only invested $163 each in Canada. (Most of the Canadian money in the U.S. tends to be in the form of "portfolio" investment which gives the investor virtually no say in the conduct of the corporation he partly owns. American holdings in Canada, on the other hand, tend to be "direct" investment, the kind that provides effective control of the affairs of the company.)

There's little doubt that Canadians, if they had the chance, would prefer to invest in Canada. We like our country and we want to share in its potentially great future. But the incredible truth is that we don't have, to the extent we should, the opportunity to invest in our own country. The Conway Report, discussed earlier, warns that there are too few Canadian investment opportunities now, and that this astounding shortage will be aggravated in future. Too many Canadian companies are closely held by private — usually meaning foreign — interests. Too few new Canadian ventures are brought to market. Too many Canadian corporations in every field of endeavour find they cannot expand because Bay Street will not help them to obtain the new capital they need.

As a last resort the Canadians then sell out to foreign interests.

Because of the appalling inadequacies of our short-sighted financial establishment, Canadian enterprises — especially outside Central Canada — are crippled for lack of capital.

A little-studied but terrifying possible consequence of the deficiencies of the Canadian capital markets is to be found in Quebec. Francophone Canadians have suffered through a century in which the English-speaking members of Canada's economic elite have shown not the slightest interest in encouraging or facilitating French-Canadian commercial enterprise. Quebec is full of foreign-owned mines and mills and the Quebecois don't like it. If, a few years from now, Quebec leaves Canada, it will be in large part because of the greed and self-defeating folly of the men on St. James Street and Bay Street.

It is time to take a closer look at the men in the broadloomed skyscraper offices in the business blocks surrounding our stock exchanges.

BAY STREET

Stand at the corner of Bay and King Streets in Toronto at noon any weekday and you will rub shoulders with the men who run Canada.

They are well-fed, well-groomed and well-dressed. They walk and talk and laugh with the kind of confidence that attaches only to men who are certain of their own power.

They're the kind of people who have a deep tan all through February.

They are also, these men who have shaped Canada to their own ends, greedy, venal, intellectually lazy, deceitful and selfish.

Overwhelmingly Anglo-Saxon in background and, nominally at least, Protestant in religious affiliation, they seem strangely detached from their racial or religious background, existing in a kind of affluent moral limbo. A year or two ago, for example, astrology became a passionate fad for at least some of these men (with heaven only knows what effect on the Canadian economy!).

They live exceedingly well. They have big, understated traditional houses in Rosedale or Forest Hill Village, weekend farms in the Caledon Hills, cottages in Muskoka or among the Ten Thousand Islands of Georgian Bay. They — and their expensively dressed and polished young wives — turn up a couple of times a year in New York and London, Switzerland, the Bahamas and Jamaica's North Shore.

They went to, and typically their children will go to, one of a handful of long-established private schools. They attended the University of Toronto or Montreal's McGill, belonged to the right fraternities, and graduated without academic distinction. They married well, usually choosing the daughters of their fathers' peers, and settled down in a business which does nothing but, in one manner or another, move money around. Often they are second- or third-generation members of the family firm.

They rise fast and soon are making decisions involving millions of dollars a day.

Their training, such as it is, is almost invariably in sales. The sophisticated technical aspects of investment tend to be left to much less powerful people — economists, analysts, researchers — who serve the investment firms but who rarely achieve real power in them. Power, in this business, is in the hands of men with the right parents, the right wife, membership in the right clubs; it is not in the hands of the men with the right brains and the right training.

And this, probably, is why the decisions made on Bay Street have been and continue to be so consistently bad. Not bad for their short-term effects on the bank accounts of the men of the economic elite. But bad, ultimately, for ordinary Canadians from coast to coast.

These powerful men are the ones who gather up money from all over Canada and decide what to do with it.

These are the men who make it not only possible but easy for foreign investors to take over Canadian companies. Talk takeover and hundreds of bright young Bay Street brokers, lawyers, accountants and salesmen will start panting with enthusiasm — there's always a fat, fast profit for them in a takeover bid.

Canadians in the money business made enormous sums by providing their services to one side or the other (or both) while two gigantic tobacco companies — one American, the

117

other South African — fought for control of Canadian Breweries, the beer colossus that E.P. Taylor had put together in the thirties by acquiring small, independent Canadian brewers. The South Africans (Rothmans) gained control of Canadian Breweries; on Bay and St. James Streets nobody reflected much on the fact that a strong, established Canadian company — and one which had become, itself, a multinational corporation by developing or acquiring subsidiaries in the U.S. and the United Kingdom — had passed into foreign hands. They were much too busy adding up the money they had made out of the fight for control to think, even in passing, about the flow of beer profits out of the country.

The Canadian Breweries caper was an archetypal Canadian financial struggle. The rich and confident men of Bay and St. James Streets went into battle on behalf of opposing foreign interests. Like the good mercenaries they are, they fought with vigour and ingenuity, knowing full well that no matter who won their own bank accounts would be fattened.

But the Canadian financial community's services to the foreigners don't stop when a takeover has been profitably completed. As soon as a new multinational presence is established in Canada, the Canadian money men go to great lengths to aid the foreigner's further growth in our country. Time and time again, financing that was denied to a Canadian company is eagerly provided for the foreign company that takes over. B-A Oil, for example, was crippled by its inability to find the funds it needed but, when Gulf Oil of Pittsburgh gained control, Canadian financial interests promptly provided one hundred million Canadian dollars to strengthen the company.

Meanwhile, of course, the Maritimes, Quebec and the West are crying for investment capital. But who on Bay Street bothers to listen to the pleas from the boondocks? Virtually, it seems, nobody. There's lots more money to be made selling Canadian corporations to foreigners as well as talking Canadians into investing their money on Wall Street. The foreigners, after all, are perfectly happy to expand their operations in Canada's East and West. Bay Street doesn't have to worry about Canada.

None of these things happens automatically. The Canadian financial community is highly structured, a sophisticated complex of companies, partnerships and public and private agencies that has evolved over the years to serve the purposes its owners, operators and creators see for it.

The major elements of the investment community might be thought of as falling into two major groupings, the money-gatherers and the money-distributors, though, as we shall see, even this simple distinction is less than completely accurate in the complex pattern of interlocking control and shifting functions of the investment community.

Predominant among the money-gatherers are the pension funds, the so-called open-end investment funds (better known as mutual funds), and two kinds of insurance companies, those that concentrate on life insurance and the fire and casualty insurance companies that write all the other kinds of policies. If you are a typical Canadian, your money is being invested through at least one, and probably several, of these "money-gatherers". Most corporations of any size at all now have pension funds to which you and your employer make regular contributions. Most Canadians also carry personal life insurance and insurance to protect their property against loss through fire, accident, theft or personal injury. And some hundreds of thousands of Canadians have invested money in the mutual funds.

The "money-distributors" are primarily the investment dealers (of which more later) and, to a much lesser extent, the broker-dealers. The investment dealers are the firms that handle the transactions whereby, for example, a pension fund uses its newly-accumulated funds to buy shares of a large, publicly-listed corporation. The broker-dealers are, typically, the firms that raise money for and provide money to smaller oil or mining exploration companies.

Investment dealers tend to run two kinds of operations at once. A large firm will have an institutional department and a retail sales department. In the institutional department, the investment dealer acts mostly as a money-distributor, finding investment opportunities for money already accumulated by a mutual fund, a pension fund or even a corporation with loose cash around. The investment dealer's institutional department will sell both common stocks (which, of course, carry no guarantees as to return on investment) and preferred stocks, bonds and debentures (which, typically, do provide guarantees of greater or lesser value that interest or dividends will actually be paid). The retail sales department will work with individual investors, handling their stock market transactions of all kinds, making recommendations of investments, and generally promoting and engaging in stock trading by individuals.

The broker-dealer is more frequently involved in "primary distribution". He sells to the public the securities of new and untried corporations, frequently in mining and oil exploration. Often no regular "auction market" exists for these securities (meaning that there is no independent system whereby buyers and sellers can get together on a price and make a trade).

Either kind of firm — investment dealer or broker-dealer — can also serve as a "money-accumulator". This happens when the dealer serves as an underwriter. The underwriter's activities, stated in the simplest possible manner, consist of guaranteeing to provide a new venture with an agreed amount of money and then selling enough shares in the venture to the public to actually produce that much money (and more: underwriters expect to make a profit).

It's worth emphasizing that most of the trading in the stock market doesn't put money in a company's treasury. When you buy a hundred shares of Inco, you aren't providing new money that Inco can use in exploring for nickel deposits. You're simply putting money in the pocket of the person who owned those hundred shares before you bought them (and, of course, into the pocket of the stock broker who handled the transaction for you). The only way that you can actually invest in Canada's growth is by buying newly-issued shares. Only when a company sells new shares does it actually benefit directly from your investment by receiving new funds that it can use for exploration, or the development of new processes, or for growth generally. I know a lady who bought shares of Atlantic Sugar at $12, thinking that she was thereby helping the company to expand into tuna fishing. But, since she was buying previously issued shares in an ordinary stock market transaction, she was putting nothing in the company's treasury. Too bad. Especially because the tuna boats couldn't find any fish and the stock eased back to about $7 a share. The company didn't benefit at all from the lady's stock purchase. But the person who sold the shares to her did. And so, inevitably, did the "customer's man" who handled the transaction for her.

In addition to money-gatherers and money-distributors, there is a third class of financial institution at work in Canada. Institutions in this class might be called "facilitators". The chartered banks fall into this category, as do the trust companies and, perhaps, the finance and acceptance companies. The banks are subject to very specific restrictions on their operations; they may or may not do certain things as prescribed by the Bank Act (which is amended every ten years or so to ensure — in theory at least — that the banks continue to provide the kind of service Canadians need). The trust companies are comparably regulated and so are the finance and acceptance companies. None of these financial institutions can be seen as either primarily money accumulators or distributors; instead they are designed to facilitate financial transactions. The banks both borrow money (in the form of deposits) and lend it, and so do the finance companies and the acceptance companies. The trust companies borrow money, but they also administer money (as trustees) and they lend it (most often as mortgages).

Just to underline the complexity of the whole situation, it's possible, for example to own shares in a Canadian bank or trust company. In such a case you are participating in the profits (if any) of the management group that operates the bank or trust company. If the managers run the business well, they will attract a lot of other people's money. The more money they attract, the more business they do and the larger the profits they make through commissions and service charges.

You might think that the same would logically follow with investment dealers, the familiar stock brokers. But it doesn't. In Canada, through a most curious anomaly, stock brokerage firms are forbidden to make public offerings of shares of their own ownership. You can buy a piece of a Canadian bank and take your chances on its fortunes, but you can't buy a piece of a Canadian investment dealer.

The investment dealers' firms are all essentially closed partnerships. In Ontario, they are required to be structured this way by the Ontario Securities Commission, which won't let them trade in stocks and bonds otherwise, and by the Toronto Stock Exchange, which won't let them use its facilities otherwise.

There is no compelling reason why the investment dealers should not be public companies, but that's the way we do things here. Your broker, if you question him on it, will probably blame the Securities Commission and the Stock Exchange. But what he neglects to tell you is that the Stock Exchange is, itself, a private club owned and run by and for its members — who happen to be those very same investment dealers — nor will he tell you that the Securities Commission, in spite of its status as a public agency, created by and responsible to the provincial government, is also in most of its actions, the willing puppet of the investment dealers and their colleagues in the financial community.

It is possible that the investment dealers don't wish to become public companies because public companies are required to reveal their sales and their profits — and because the officers of public companies are required to act always on behalf of their shareholders.

The Montreal Stock Exchange was first organized, with less than a dozen members, in 1832. Among the issues that traded on the first day were shares in Canada's first railway, the Champlain and St. Lawrence. The Toronto Exchange followed on October 24, 1852, with trading limited to one half hour each morning. In the early years, the exchanges were quiet places (you paid $5 for a seat on the exchange in Toronto) and didn't seem to be the fast road to riches. But that changed late in the nineteenth century. In 1896, a group of traders who were interested in the stocks of Canadian mining companies — which had been neglected by the Toronto Stock Exchange — formed an exchange of their own, the Toronto Stock and Mining Exchange. Almost at once a third exchange opened in Toronto, the Standard Stock and Mining Exchange, but the two new exchanges merged in 1899 under the Standard name.

Toronto Stock Exchange members initially looked down on the Standard Exchange; trade in speculative mining shares was somehow less than respectable and the members of the TSE believed in respectability. However they believed even more in profit and they were chagrined to see the success of some of the companies traded on the Standard Exchange — and the profits that arose from trading their shares. So the Toronto Stock Exchange began to go after mining listings and a bitter rivalry developed between the two exchanges.

The rivalry ended in 1934 when the Standard Exchange was merged — with Ontario government encouragement — into the Toronto Stock Exchange. The respectable investment dealers of the Toronto Stock Exchange, members of the economic elite, had succeeded in taking over the less respectable, maverick organization which had done so much to stimulate the development of Canadian mining.

The Toronto Stock Exchange, once it had absorbed the Standard Exchange, began in the following decades to lose interest in the natural resource industries. When the fastest profits were in mining, TSE members were interested in mining. But when the Canadian economy matured, when inter-listings with New York became more common, when foreign funds began to flow into Canadian industry in substantial quantities, trading in speculative mining securities was actively discouraged by the TSE. By the beginning of the seventies, TSE members had to consult a map to find Cobalt.

Time was when every purchase through every stock exchange was a wild, blind speculation. But somehow members of the Toronto Stock Exchange have managed to instill a strange distinction in the minds of investors in the last two decades. Under "people's capitalism" investment in unproven industrial ventures was all right — in fact, the royal road to riches for the average citizen — but investment in speculative mines or oils was the height of folly and involved a quick slide to ruin. The TSE members seem to have picked up this curious idea from their counterparts and mentors in New York.

But it was in New York that Brunswick Corporation (bowling alleys) traded at almost $75 in 1960-61 and at $6 in 1966, Kalvar Corporation (desalinization of water) went in the same period from $706 a share to $35 and dozens of other companies took equally precipitous drops.

Toronto tended to follow the New York example with a little delay. So let's look at a few recent share prices on the TSE. Dylex Diversified, for example, the reorganized successor to Tip-Top Tailors: $40.25 in 1969 and $3.75 in 1970. Or Harvey's Foods (who still make good hamburgers, which must stick in the throats of some speculators) which went from

$12.50 a share in 1969 to a low of 57¢ a share in 1970. Or Seaway Multi-Corp., an incredible adventure in creative capitalism in which an enterprising promoter named Norton Cooper combined bicyles and hotels and auto parts and Italian shoes into a "mini-conglomerate", and saw the company's shares hit $36.75 before sinking back to $3.75 (the full story of this particular bit of Canadian industrial history remains to be told — disasters are rarely described in detail on Bay Street.)

Again, in the market "adjustment" from 1969 highs to 1970 lows, Computel Systems went from $45.00 to $3.25, OSF Industries went from $34.50 to $2.50, and Riley's Datashare went from an even $20.00 to an even $1.00 a share.

If a Canadian investor had followed brokers' recommendations and acquired one share of each of seventeen highly touted Canadian "junior industrials" in 1969, he would have paid $395.46 for his acquisitions. But if his bank manager had forced him to sell these same shares at their 1970 lows (and a lot of bank managers forced a lot of their customers to do just that), the value of the same portfolio would have been $36.57, for a loss of around ninety percent.

The established investment dealers had come a long way in three-quarters of a century. From dealing sedately in government bonds and a few respectable industrials (Bell Telephone, CPR, the Hudson's Bay Company) in the nineteenth century they moved in on Canada's mining boom, reaped a rich profit, lost interest in mining and natural resources generally and became, most recently, enamoured with junior industrials.

After the TSE and the Montreal Exchange lost interest in natural resources, a concentrated and sustained smear campaign was directed at the mining developers, speculators and broker-dealers who were still attempting, on the fringes of the financial establishment, to find mines and strike oil. Conveniently overlooked, however, was the fact that investors were able to lose money just as fast on Toronto-sponsored junior industrials like Facs Limited (computer and "instant printing" franchises) as on the most barren and desolate piece of muskeg or moose pasture.

But Toronto's recurring passion for junior industrials was not a home-grown phenomenon. It reflected, instead, the fads and fashions of Wall Street. The personal and financial links between the Canadian economic elite and the money masters of Wall Street have been growing for generations. More and more our future has been integrated with that of the United States.

Canadian mutual funds, by 1967, had invested 53% of the money entrusted to them by Canadian investors in foreign securities (when, you will recall, Canadian politicians, economists and businessmen were eagerly seeking foreign money because we were, allegedly, deficient in new investment capital). Investment decisions by mutual funds are made by the funds' professional managers who are, of course, members of the same community as the investment dealers, analysts and salesmen who make recommendations to the funds.

By the spring of 1971, when the Ontario Government reacted — belatedly — to the threat that New York firms would completely take over the securities industry in Canada, no fewer than nine member firms of the Toronto Stock Exchange were "non-resident controlled". The list included such U.S. giants as Bache & Co. and Merrill Lynch, Pierce, Fenner & Smith of Canada Ltd. Merrill Lynch has a capital base of $360 million, as compared to $14 million for Wood Gundy Securities Ltd., the largest Canadian-owned investment house. For Merrill Lynch and most, if not all, of the other American-owned firms, investors' money is seen as naturally flowing to Wall Street. And it usually does.

The new Ontario regulations, imposed in the middle of July, also restricted further non-resident ownership of firms that "distribute" (i.e. sell) mutual funds. At the time the regulations were enacted the *Financial Post* recorded that twenty-two Canadian mutual funds were controlled by non-residents (not all American, it should be added; the list includes six funds operated by I.O.S. of Canada Limited, the Canadian manifestation of the razzle-dazzle, jet-set Swiss-based financial empire created by Bernie Cornfeld, so unsavoury a complex that it isn't even allowed to be operated in the United States).

In spite of the welcome mat spread out for foreign firms, and in spite of the fact that the Toronto Stock Exchange dominates the market for Canadian listed stocks with 96% of market value of all listed stocks (this includes interlistings with other exchanges), Toronto has recently been losing ground among North American stock exchanges. In 1969, Toronto was the continent's fourth busiest exchanges, but in 1970 it was fifth. The dollar value of trading in Toronto fell to $3.7 billion in 1970 from $5.8 billion in 1969 and Toronto's place was taken by the Pacific Coast Exchange. It is no surprise that the New York Stock Exchange held down the number one spot with — even in the disastrous trading of 1970 — a turnover of $103 billion worth of shares.

Resented as it is — and with good reason — in other parts of the country, the truth is that as Toronto goes, so goes the nation — at least in the securities business. Montreal has faded to a distant second. The Maritimes have no exchange of their own and investment firms in the Atlantic provinces have either dissolved or been taken over or merged into the large firms from Central Canada.

In the west only the Vancouver Exchange — young, rambunctious, exciting and speculation-oriented — maintains any noticeable independence of the Toronto and Montreal economic elite. And it's highly significant that British Columbia is the only province in Canada in which Canadians still own more than half of both their manufacturing and natural resources industries. In mining, only 26.7% was controlled by foreigners in B.C. in 1968 as compared to 59.3% foreign control in Ontario, 88.8% in the Maritimes and 40.6% in Quebec. In Ontario 70.0% of manufacturing was foreign controlled; comparable figures in the Maritimes were 59.6%, in Quebec 60.3% and on the Prairies 60.5%, but only (only!) 44.1% of British Columbia's manufacturing was foreign controlled.

Vancouver is the one bright spot in an otherwise gloomy picture. The TSE's domination of Canadian stock trading has not only had the effect of eclipsing — or preventing the creation of — other exchanges in other parts of the country, it has also produced a concentration of power in the hands of a small, cliquish group of large investment dealers. This is a process which has been going on for many years, but it has become virtually complete in the last decade.

Ten years ago at least seventy out of roughly a hundred active members of the TSE were raising new capital for Canadian corporations in the resource industries. Today none of the member firms is doing so. Regulations of the Ontario Securities Commission, endorsed by the large investment firms that dominate the Toronto Stock Exchange, have made it virtually impossible to raise money for resource development.

Ironically, one of the most highly-respected leaders of the American financial community recently emphasized the importance of smaller firms willing to underwrite new ventures. William McChesney Martin Jr., who became president of the New York Stock Exchange at the age of 31 in 1938 and who subsequently spent 19 years as chairman of the Federal Reserve Board, states in a study for the NYSE that the success with which new capital has been raised to finance the American economy is due in part to the dispersion and local activities of a multitude of broker-dealers and he urges that any changes in the structure of the investment business in the U.S. should not hurt the efficient small firms.

The National Association of Security Dealers in the U.S.

has about 5,000 members scattered all across the country, and these firms have been responsible for raising between 75% and 80% of all new equity investment in that country.

These NASD firms, which Martin says are essential to a healthy economy, are the direct counterparts of the smaller Canadian firms which the overlords of the TSE have squeezed out of the Canadian securities business.

Meanwhile, back on Bay Street, the beautifully-groomed denizen goes through his day. Sell a Canadian company in the morning. A dry martini and a small, rare steak at lunch. Persuade a big "money-collector" to invest in an American company in the afternoon. Home to the newspaper, two highballs, three neat children and a wife who is beginning to get a small crease across the forehead. Dinner served by the West Indian maid (he pays her less a month than he earns a day). And an evening with the charts and the financial papers, broken only by a family discussion about which continent this year's skiing should be done on.

It is sad that this man and a thousand others just like him are destroying Canada's future and depriving Canadians of their heritage.

It is even sadder that he isn't even doing as well as he might for himself in the process. He is a member of the economic elite of a nation that contains the world's greatest treasury of increasingly scarce natural resources. Abstracted, dessicated, de-materialized, the materials of industrial society pass across his desk every day — oil and gas, iron ore, new machines and new processes, exotic space age minerals — but he doesn't see them as they are, the life blood of industrialized society. Instead, they appear as dollar signs. A quick trading profit. That's what they get when they sell Canada across their polished desks. But they don't understand they're selling too cheap. They're too eager to sell today, take the trading profit right now. They're reluctant to place their faith in the riches of the Canadian land and the energy of the Canadian people —

better, they think, to sell now before the market for Canada collapses.

But they — and we — would be richer in the long run if they weren't so eager to sell fast. There's no need to transfer ownership of our resources to foreigners. Keep the means of production at home and sell the products. In the long run we benefit enormously and non-Canadians lose very little.

This kind of logic, however, is not part of the folk wisdom of Bay Street. The fast buck dominates all the decisions, and the long-range interests of Canadians — or even of the next generation of the economic elite — don't enter into the decision-making process.

Clearly — though unfortunately — we cannot let good sense and free enterprise solve the problem, because they've demonstrated repeatedly that they cannot cope with the strange aberrations of Canadian society and the Canadian economy. Instead, government — meaning public — action is necessary. We must, collectively and through conscious decision as expressed in legislation, express our will.

The men of Bay and St. James Streets have had their chance. For a century we have entrusted to them the determination of the direction of the Canadian economy. They have been tried, and they have been found wanting. Now other solutions, other institutions, must be tried.

And that is the subject of the next and final chapter.

THE GATES OF INNOVATION

Chronic unemployment. Steadily rising living costs. Export industries that are in danger of pricing themselves out of world markets. An ominously increasing direct foreign control of key sections of our economy. Provinces competing with each other to attract additional foreign investment while Canadian savings flow out of the country. And three thousand miles of undefended border with the world's paramount imperial power which is seeking, with increasing urgency, "secure" sources of energy and raw materials to meet its insatiable requirements.

As these things go, Canada's past has been a happy one. But the available evidence indicates that our future is going to be neither so happy, nor so full of promise as we had expected.

Unless we act now. Unless we throw open the gates of innovation, recognize that old solutions aren't good enough for new problems, and begin at once, consciously and deliberately, to create the conditions in which Canadians can once again control their own future.

None of this will be easy. Innovation never is. For any positive programme of national rehabilitation there will be objections and obstacles. The programme will be impractical, too expensive, too visionary. The people will never stand for it. It won't work. It will be opposed by big business, or big labour, or consumers, or academics, or left, or right, or centre.

We won't want to face the repercussions that will be introduced by foreign economic interests — or Canadian financial ones. The people won't vote for any politician who supports a program of national rehabilitation — and they certainly won't elect a government that embraces such a programme.

And yet, if you have accepted only part of the argument of this book, only a portion of the evidence presented, then you will recognize that we must innovate. Now.

What follows is in no sense a complete programme. It is, in fact, only the barest outline, an indicator, a series of very gentle hints, much more tentative than indicative. It would be presumptuous folly for any one person to believe that he could spell out in detail the collective decisions to be taken by twenty million others.

But still, I believe the points that follow are useful. In one way or another they must be implemented; modified, improved upon, expanded but, in the ultimate sense implemented. eight points, then.

First. Because it has been mentioned earlier, a Maritimes Stock Exchange. A useful thing in itself — desperately needed by the capital-starved Atlantic Provinces — but even more useful as a demonstration. If we create a viable stock exchange east of Montreal, then we will give the natural energy of the citizens of Atlantic Canada a chance to rennovate their own economy. New, local capital pumped into natural resources and into manufacturing and other industry could radically alter the circumstances of the East. Federal and provincial governments have been spending vast sums of money in an effort to provide Maritimers with some approximation of the opportunities and rewards that are available to other Canadians. Private initiative and private capital, channeled through a local financial institution oriented to local needs, could replace much of the public effort, and could probably do so at lower real cost and with higher real rewards.

Government of course would benefit in other ways from a

healthier economy in the Atlantic Provinces. The fiscal demand on Ottawa would decrease as employment and incomes rose. And local governments, both provincial and municipal, would be better able to pay for the services that Canadians expect and are entitled to.

But a Maritimes stock exchange would demonstrate — perhaps conclusively — that the total Canadian economy need not, and indeed should not, be dependent upon the handful of inadequate men who man the financial establishment in Central Canada.

Break the hold of Bay Street and St. James Street on the Canadian economy and you raise the possibility that long-neglected regions of the nation might experience a startling economic renaissance.

Second. Comprehensive, blanket legislation to ensure that no new natural resource company be allowed to form or operate in Canada unless its voting stock is 80% owned by Canadians.

We have already acted in this field, hesitantly, timidly and without any clear sense of direction. The Federal Government created Panarctic Oil. It stopped Steve Roman from selling his controlling interest in Dennison Mines to foreign buyers. It stopped a comparable sell-out of Home Oil. The latter two decisions at least were in response to an urgent and immediately critical situation; government acted from a gut-feeling for what Canadians wanted, not from a clearly formulated general policy. (In late 1970 and through the first half of 1971, the Hon. Herb Gray, Minister of National Revenue, worked on a Cabinet assignment to formulate just such a policy; at this writing we have no way of knowing what recommendations will be made, or what will be accepted, but the government clearly deserves credit for recognizing that our past approach to the problem of increasing foreign control of our resource industries was inadequate).

New resource ventures should be able to sell abroad as

many preferred shares, bonds and debentures as are consistent with a company's needs and the state of the Canadian dollar. But voting control must remain in Canada. We suggest the 80% figure for Canadian ownership because anything less makes foreign control entirely possible — and, in fact, likely in many instances. 51% Canadian ownership, for example, means very little if the 51% is spread over thousands of individual investors, trustees, pension funds, mutual funds and other "portfolio" investors while 49% is closely held in one pair of foreign hands. In such an instance, the 49% clearly controls the venture, elects the directors, appoints the officers, and determines the company's programme. Thus, 80% in Canadian hands. This still doesn't eliminate the possibility of foreign control — but it does make it significantly more difficult.

Third. Additional controls in the form of an equalization tax on the export of Canadian capital. Canada is rare — almost unique — among the capital-accumulating nations in its lack of controls over the flow of its money out of the country. Other things being equal, the free flow of funds across national boundaries would, in the long run, work to everybody's benefit. But other things, unfortunately, are not equal. Most of the capital we export ends up as "portfolio" investment in the United States, while the capital we import, overwhelmingly from the United States but from Britain and Europe too, takes the form of "direct" investment in Canadian resources and Canadian industry, removing control of significant portions of our economy from our own hands. *Laissez-faire*-minded readers will find the thought of controls on the flow of capital repugnant at first glance. They should reflect on the increasingly-apparent alternative — growing government control over the activities of the foreign-owned corporations. If we keep our money at home, our growing economy's capital needs will be met by Canadian funds. If that happens, the rate of alienation of our industries will slow down. And a reduction in the encroachments of foreign control on the economy will reduce the need for detailed government legislation and regulation designed to force the foreign-owned corporations to be good Canadian "corporate citizens". Anyone who has followed events of the past few years will recognize that we have already made up our minds to try to limit the importance of foreign decision-making power over our economy; so far we have gone about this by harrassing the foreign-owned corporations with government regulations. How much better it would be to ensure that the corporations remained in Canadian hands in the first place.

Fourth. Tax incentives and penalties to encourage the extractive industries to reinvest a meaningful proportion of their profits in secondary industry and other developmental initiatives in the regions from which they are taking their profits in the first place. As matters now stand, depreciation and depletion allowances provide our petroleum and mining industries with tax benefits that are not enjoyed by other forms of enterprise. The original rationale behind this is sensible enough; a mine or an oil field has a limited economic life so the companies digging the ore or pumping the petroleum must receive appropriate tax concessions if they are to survive to find other mines, other oil wells. But in practice the special concessions allowed the natural resource companies have produced great scars on the Canadian landscape and have blighted the lives of tens of thousands of individual Canadians. An exploitable ore body is found. A mine is dug and a mill built. A town springs up and flourishes for twenty years. Then the ore body is exhausted, the mine is closed, and the town rots away. For the miners and their families, and for the merchants and service personnel who helped create the community that depended upon the mine, the death of the major local industry produces hardship, suffering and the kind of dislocation of their lives that many never really recover from. Our traditional approach to this problem has allowed the companies to survive, but it has killed the communities. Dawson City has been a ghost town for seventy years. Cape Breton suffers acutely from the closing of the mines. Ontario, from Sudbury to the Soo, has perhaps twenty years before it encounters the same problems as Cape Breton. And, on a larger scale, the Province of Alberta faces within the foreseeable future an end to the oil bonanza as petroleum exploration and development moves north and the prairie province's reserves and revenues drop. This need not be so. These areas need not be totally dependent upon the transient benefits brought by the extractive industries. But to develop their other, more permanent, potentials, investment capital is needed. If funds were diverted from the cash flow of the extractive industries into more permanent enterprises the regions themselves would benefit and so, ultimately, would Canada as a whole. North-Central Ontario, for example, has the potential to become the nation's heavy industry heartland with its ready access to power, steel and cheap, water-borne transportation. Alberta is woefully dependent upon petroleum now but could, with its comparatively easy access to the Pacific and the booming American Northwest, develop enough secondary industry to make its present prosperity permanent. And, painting with an even broader brush, it's possible to visualize the financing and development of Richard Rohmer's visionary Mid-Canada Corridor from the profits of mineral and petroleum exploitation in our Mid-North and Arctic (the Mid-Canada Corridor is a broad band of proposed development which starts in Labrador, arcs gently across northern Quebec, Ontario, Manitoba and Saskatchewan and then up the Mackenzie Valley to the Arctic Coast. The Corridor generally includes that part of Canada which is now virtually deserted but which is nevertheless below the tree line and blessed with a liveable climate.)

Fifth. A more vigorous assertion of our sovereignty in the Canadian North and a more orderly exploitation of the

North's resources. It is hard to see a more meaningful role for Canada's Armed Forces than that they might play in maintaining a significant Canadian presence in the North. We have taken steps in this direction in recent years — there is now a permanent contingent of the Armed Forces stationed in Yellowknife (almost thirty men!) — and more needs to be done.

Sixth. Federal and provincial programmes to encourage the growth of industry in under-developed parts of the country should be strictly and severely limited to companies owned and controlled in Canada. It is grotesque to see provinces competing with each other to give money or forgiveable loans to giant multinational corporations in order to woo them into establishing branch plants. It is equally grotesque to see the federal government spending your money and mine to advertise in *Fortune,* the magazine of the American business establishment, that companies can receive $30,000 for every job they create by opening new plants in Canada. Incentives of this kind, if properly used, do have a role to play in reducing regional disparities in Canada (we shouldn't have all our factories in the belt from Windsor to Montreal; this is bad not only for economic but for social and environmental reasons as well), but there is no real justification for providing these incentives to rich, multinational firms. Does IBM really need subsidies from the Canadian taxpayer's pocket? The answer is clearly no. But new and growing Canadian-owned firms, traditionally capital-starved, can use assistance of this kind.

Seventh. Foreign-owned firms must be obliged to conform fully to Canadian laws. Because of the workings of the Americans' Trading With the Enemy Act, Canadian firms have, in the past, been unable to sell trucks to China or mill flour for Cuba. Recent instances of such blatant encroachments on our sovereignty have not been nearly so dramatic, but as the U.S. struggles to bolster its economy and its currency against

their current deterioration, we can expect orders or sugges-
tions from Washington officials to the firms that control the
branch plants in Canada. Corporate charters, whether provincial or federal, are granted at the discretion of government. They should be revoked for any firms which are clearly
altering their Canadian operations or policies to conform
with non-Canadian legal requirements.

Eighth. A deliberate expansion of our commitment to
scientific and technological research and innovation. We have
demonstrated in the past our ability to innovate as effectively
as any people on the face of the earth. We have been world
leaders in the development of geological surveying and in
mining technology. Canadian medical research has, from
time to time, achieved enormously important breakthroughs,
from insulin to the electron microscope. We are alone in the
world in the development of nuclear power reactors fueled
with natural uranium (there is, at the moment, a vigorous
debate going on as to whether our nuclear programme is on
the right track, but right or wrong it does demonstrate that
we are capable of competing in the most advanced and esoteric
fields of modern technology). Clearly, with just over 20
million people we cannot expect to match the across-the-board
research and development capabilities of the US or the
USSR, or even Europe or Japan. But we can, if we choose our
ground carefully and intelligently, achieve permanent world
leadership in selected fields. Switzerland has neither the
population, nor the income, nor the resources, both natural
and of highly educated citizens, that we have, but the Swiss
have achieved undisputed world leadership in the creation and
production of pharmaceuticals. The Swedes might have been
content to remain iron miners because their country is blessed
with rich ore deposits, but they have used their resource
base to become world leaders in the production of indispen-
sible ball bearings and of such other high-technology products
as automobiles and military aircraft. At present we produce

raw materials for export and we manufacture — in our branch plants — slavish copies of foreign-designed and created products. This is a fragile base on which to build a strong, mature economy and it is why we are the world's richest under-developed nation. In the long run, patents, processes and the sophisticated, highly-trained manpower that can function at the forefront of technology are more important to us than nickel mines or gas wells. Because so much of our industry is in foreign hands, disgracefully little original or applied research is now carried on in Canada by industry — the foreign-owned companies do their research at home — either directly or through the provision of earmarked funds for universities or other research-oriented establishments. Innovative research in Canada has become, by default, a responsibility of government. Until we repatriate our economy, government must continue to discharge that responsibility.

Obliged as we are to get up every morning and meet each day's problems, we pay too little heed to the future. But many of the readers of this book will live to see the Twenty-First Century — and some of the great-grandchildren you will meet before you die will live into the Twenty-Second Century. Just as we accept responsibility for our contemporaries, so too we should give thought for the human beings — our own descendents — who will come after us. The decisions we make now will alter the lives of generations unborn and unimagined. If we want our children and our grandchildren and our great grandchildren to live lives of hope and fulfillment, then we must act now to direct the future.

The members of the Canadian economic establishment have developed a system that enables them to preserve their power and their wealth from one generation to another. They have done so to the great detriment of you and me and Canada.

And that is what we must change. Now.

FOR FURTHER READING

Here is a short list of other books that will provide you with more information on the topics covered in *Sold American!* You should be able to find all these titles in your local book store or public library. If you cannot find the book you are looking for, ask for it. Your book store can order a copy for you if the book isn't in stock, and your public library can quickly obtain a copy through Canada's efficient inter-library loan system.

THE VERTICAL MOSAIC by John Porter. This is the first and so far the only real study of the power structure of Canadian society. Professor Porter's description of the economic elite and its strength is particularly important. Essential reading. University of Toronto Press, Toronto, 1965. Paperbound. $4.50

SILENT SURRENDER by Kari Levitt. Miss Levitt's landmark study demonstrates the alienation of the Canadian economy with a massive and impressive collection of facts and statistics from previously little-known sources. This book has become the Bible of the economic nationalists and deservedly so. Macmillan Company of Canada, Toronto, 1970. Paperbound. $3.95

THE SUPPLY OF, AND DEMAND FOR, CANADIAN EQUITIES. This is the famous Conway Report, commissioned and published by the Toronto Stock Exchange. A careful reading of the Conway Report reveals just how grossly distorted the pattern of Canadian investment has become. Toronto Stock Exchange, Toronto, 1970. Two paperbound volumes. $20.00 (A "Conspectus" — a kind of summary of the Report's findings — is also available from the T.S.E. Paperbound. $2.00)

FROM GORDON TO WATKINS TO YOU. An interesting collection of documents and personal essays in support of economic and cultural nationalism. Mel Watkins' own account of how he changed his views from continentalism to economic nationalism is fascinating. New Press, Toronto, 1970. Paper-bound. $3.50

THE STAR-SPANGLED BEAVER edited by John H. Redekop. A collection of twenty-four papers by everybody from Mel Watkins to John Diefenbaker on the U.S. and Canada-U.S. relations. Unlike most recent Canadian books, this one is not wholly committed to the economic nationalist viewpoint; several writers make a vigourous case for closer relations with the U.S. Peter Martin Associates, Toronto, 1971. Clothbound. $8.95

THE ENERGY POKER GAME by James Laxer. A short, fierce and very important argument about the dangers inherent in making a continental energy resources deal with the United States. New Press, Toronto, 1970. Paperbound. $1.50

THE MINE FINDERS by George Lomm. A big, illustrated collection of stories about Canadian mining men and their discoveries. Non-technical and frequently entertaining. Pitt Publishing Company Limited, Toronto, 1966. Clothbound. $4.95 (Pitt Publishing has produced several popular books about Canadian mining. Write to them for a free catalogue at 77 York Street, Toronto.)

THE WALL STREET JUNGLE by Richard Ney. This book is perhaps a little cranky. Mr. Ney blames the fleecing you are likely to get in the Market on the operations of the "special-ists". But he also has a lot of interesting things to say about the cosy, club-like nature of the Stock Exchanges and the agencies that are meant to regulate them. Grove Press, New York, 1970. Paperbound. $1.50

LIVING IN THE SEVENTIES edited by Allen M. Linden. A collection of papers presented for discussion at the Liberal Party's Harrison Conference at the end of 1969. Only a few of the essays deal specifically with economic problems, but taken together they provide a picture of the challenges facing

Canada in this decade. Peter Martin Associates, Toronto, 1970. Paperbound. $3.95

RECLAIMING THE CANADIAN ECONOMY by Gunnar Adler-Karlsson. Sweden might have been as foreign-dominated as Canada, but it isn't. This interesting little book from Sweden has real relevance for Canadians. With an introduction by Abraham Rotstein. House of Anansi, Toronto, 1970. Paperbound. $1.75

THE STOCK PROMOTION BUSINESS by Ivan Shaffer. A lively, if somewhat one-sided account of how promoters use speculative greed to line their own pockets. McClelland and Stewart, Toronto, 1967. Paperbound. $2.50

A CHOICE FOR CANADA by Walter L. Gordon. This little book gives a clear and straightforward picture of Mr. Gordon's views. Although a little dated now, it is still highly relevant. McClelland and Stewart, Toronto, 1966. Paperbound, out of print. Clothbound, $4.50

APPENDIX

OUR POSITION IN FIGURES

Discussions of dollar amounts exceeding $100,000 have little meaning for most of us; they are amounts which are simply beyond ready comprehension. To bring enormous sums into perspective, remember that a million dollars is less than 5¢ for every Canadian, and a billion dollars is about $45.00 for each of us.

To provide a framework for the following figures, here is Canada's GNP (Gross National Product) for several years. GNP is the value of goods and services produced in Canada each year and it provides a yardstick against which amounts in the other tables can be measured. Our payout of dividends to foreign owners is shown in comparison.

TABLE I
A MEASURE OF THE NATION'S BUSINESS
(in millions of dollars)

	1935	1940	1945	1950
GNP	4,301	6,713	11,863	17,995
Dividends paid to non-residents	120	182	138	404

	1955	1960	1965	1968
GNP	27,895	37,775	54,897	71,454
Dividends	394	493	815	876

The most basic measure of Canada's international financial position is contained in the next table:

TABLE II
CANADIAN BALANCE OF INTERNATIONAL PAYMENTS
(in millions of dollars)

	1935	1940	1945	1950	1955	1960	1965	1968
Merchandise: Exports	732	1,202	3,474	3,139	4,332	5,392	8,745	14,874
Imports	526	1,006	1,442	3,132	4,543	5,540	8,627	13,987
Balance	206	196	2,032	7	-211	-148	118	887
Non-Merchandise:								
Receipts(1)	413	574	982	1,148	1,749	1,787	2,719	4,048
Payments(2)	494	621	1,468	1,474	2,225	2,872	3,920	5,726
Balance	-81	-47	-486	-326	-476	-1,085	-1,201	-1,678
Current Account:								
Balance	123	149	1,546	-319	-687	-1,233	-1,083	-791
Net capital movements:								
Long-term forms(3)				610	414	929	713	2,162
Short-term forms(4)				431	229	265	527	-1,375
Total	-152	-188	-693	1,041	643	1,194	1,240	787

(1) includes gold production available for export, travel expenditures, interest and dividends, freight and shipping, inheritances and immigrants' funds

(2) includes travel, interest and dividends, freight and shipping, inheritances and emigrants' funds, official contributions.

(3) includes direct investments, trade in outstanding securities, new issues and retirements (Canadian and foreign), loans, capital subscriptions, etc., by the Canadian government and export credits at the risk of the Canadian government

(4) includes change in Canadian dollar holdings of foreigners, Canadian commercial and finance company paper, etc.

145

In November, 1970, the *Survey of Current Business,* an official U.S. government publication, presented valuable new information on how U.S. corporations operating abroad in various countries are financed. The study covered only three areas of economic activity — mining and smelting, the petroleum industry, and manufacturing — so it isn't really comprehensive. It does, however, present a vivid picture of the way in which American companies operating abroad rely on local sources for the bulk of their financing (in only one of the years studied did new funds from the U.S. exceed 20% of the total new financing of the American corporations operating outside the U.S.).

In the table that follows, we present the basic figures for the financing of U.S. corporations operating in Canada.

TABLE III
SOURCES OF FUNDS FOR U.S. SUBSIDIARIES
AND AFFILIATES IN CANADA
(in millions of dollars)

Year	Total New Funds	New Funds from U.S.	New funds from U.S. as percent of total
1963	1,666	168	10.1%
1964	2,038	156	7.6
1965	2,656	551	20.8
1967	2,527	242	9.6
1968	2,611	127	4.9

In 1968, U.S. corporations operating in Canada obtained $1,027,000,000 in new money from net income, $864,000,000 from depreciation and depletion, $529,000,000 in "funds obtained abroad" (presumably almost exclusively from Canadian sources), $138,000,000 from "other sources and adjustments", and only $127,000,000 in new money flowing to Canada from the U.S. In the same year, the same corporations paid out $498,000,000, of which it is safe to assume that at least half, or $249,000,000, was returned to the United States.

A similar survey conducted by the Department of Industry, Trade and Commerce presents additional information. It is, however, important to note the different bases used in this Canadian study as compared to the U.S. *Survey of Current Business* figures presented opposite.

The Canadian survey covers all industrial groupings; the U.S. survey is limited to mining and smelting, petroleum, and manufacturing. The U.S. survey covers only 450 companies in all parts of the world and doesn't report how many of these firms operate in Canada. The Canadian survey covers non-financial companies incorporated in Canada with assets exceeding $5 million and with voting shares more than 50% held by a non-resident corporation.

Because many of the 326 companies reporting in the Canadian study consolidated information from several affiliates and subsidiaries, the results actually reflect the operations of 972 individual companies. These had, among them, total sales of $15.3 billion in 1964 and $20.7 billion in 1967. This volume of business is about one-quarter of the business carried on by all non-financial, non-government corporations in Canada.

Finally, the preceding U.S. report covers only U.S. companies, while the Canadian figures deal with firms controlled in a number of foreign countries.

Note that the Canadian report covers only firms in which over 50% of the voting stock is held by foreigners. It is possible to control a company by holding far less than 50% of its stock and there are an unknown number of foreign-controlled companies active in Canada which are not documented in this study.

The next four tables are derived from the Canadian study.

TABLE IV
PERFORMANCE OF
FOREIGN-CONTROLLED COMPANIES IN CANADA
(in millions of dollars)

	1964	1965	1966	1967
Income:				
From Sales in Canada	12,492	14,057	15,311	16,143
From export sales	2,850	3,074	3,949	4,599
Total	15,342	17,131	19,260	20,742
Other receipts	305	383	413	415
Total income	15,647	17,514	19,673	21,157
Value of total Canadian exports	8,238	8,745	10,326	11,338
Exports of foreign-controlled companies as % of total Canadian exports	35%	35%	38%	41%

TABLE V
PROFITS OF
FOREIGN-CONTROLLED COMPANIES IN CANADA
(in millions of dollars)

	1964	1965	1966	1967
Total Income	15,657	17,514	19,673	21,157
Total Expenses	13,535	15,202	17,284	18,757
Operating profit	2,112	2,311	2,389	2,400
Less:				
Income Tax Provision	593	638	648	628
Other, including depreciation	711	828	831	894
Net profit	808	845	910	877
Dividends declared	385	425	459	371
Retained earnings	423	420	451	506

TABLE VI
DIVIDENDS DECLARED BY
FOREIGN-CONTROLLED COMPANIES IN CANADA
BY RESIDENCE OF PAYEE
(in millions of dollars)

	1964	1965	1966	1967
To residents of:				
U.S.	307	336	367	272
Other foreign	42	45	46	47
Canada	36	44	46	52

TABLE VII
FINANCING OF
FOREIGN-CONTROLLED COMPANIES IN CANADA
(in millions of dollars)

	1965	1966	1967
Current retained earnings	420	451	506
Depreciation and similar sources	828	831	894
Total generated internally	1,248	1.282	1.400
Net funds from borrowing and sale of equities	780	734	581
Total new funds available	2,028	2.016	1.981

TABLE VIII
GEOGRAPHICAL ORIGIN OF
NET EXTERNAL FUNDS OF FOREIGN-CONTROLLED
COMPANIES IN CANADA
(in millions of dollars)

	1965	1966	1967
From the U.S.:			
Parents and affiliates	410	342	200
Other sources	147	107	−3
Total from U.S.	557	449	197
From other foreign:			
Parents and affiliates	6	12	7
Other sources	−3	5	3
Total from other foreign	3	17	10
From Canada:			
Parents and affiliates	40	−11	4
Other	180	279	370
Total from Canada	220	268	374
Total from all sources	780	734	581

Finally, here is a table that indicates the role that Canadian public funds play in the financing of foreign-controlled companies in Canada. These figures are from Ontario, but comparable figures could be presented from, for example, Manitoba, Quebec, Nova Scotia and Ottawa.

TABLE IX
ONTARIO DEVELOPMENT CORPORATION LOANS
FROM INCEPTION TO MARCH 31, 1970
BY NATIONALITY OF RECIPIENT COMPANY

	No. of Loans	Total Amount	Percentage of Total No.	Amount
Loans to:				
Canadian companies	136	$17,133,000	58.9%	48.7%
U.S. companies	74	13,665,000	32.0	38.8
Other foreign companies	21	4,408,000	9.1	12.5
Totals	231	35,206,000	100.0%	100.0%